Qu Leilei
A Chinese Artist in Britain

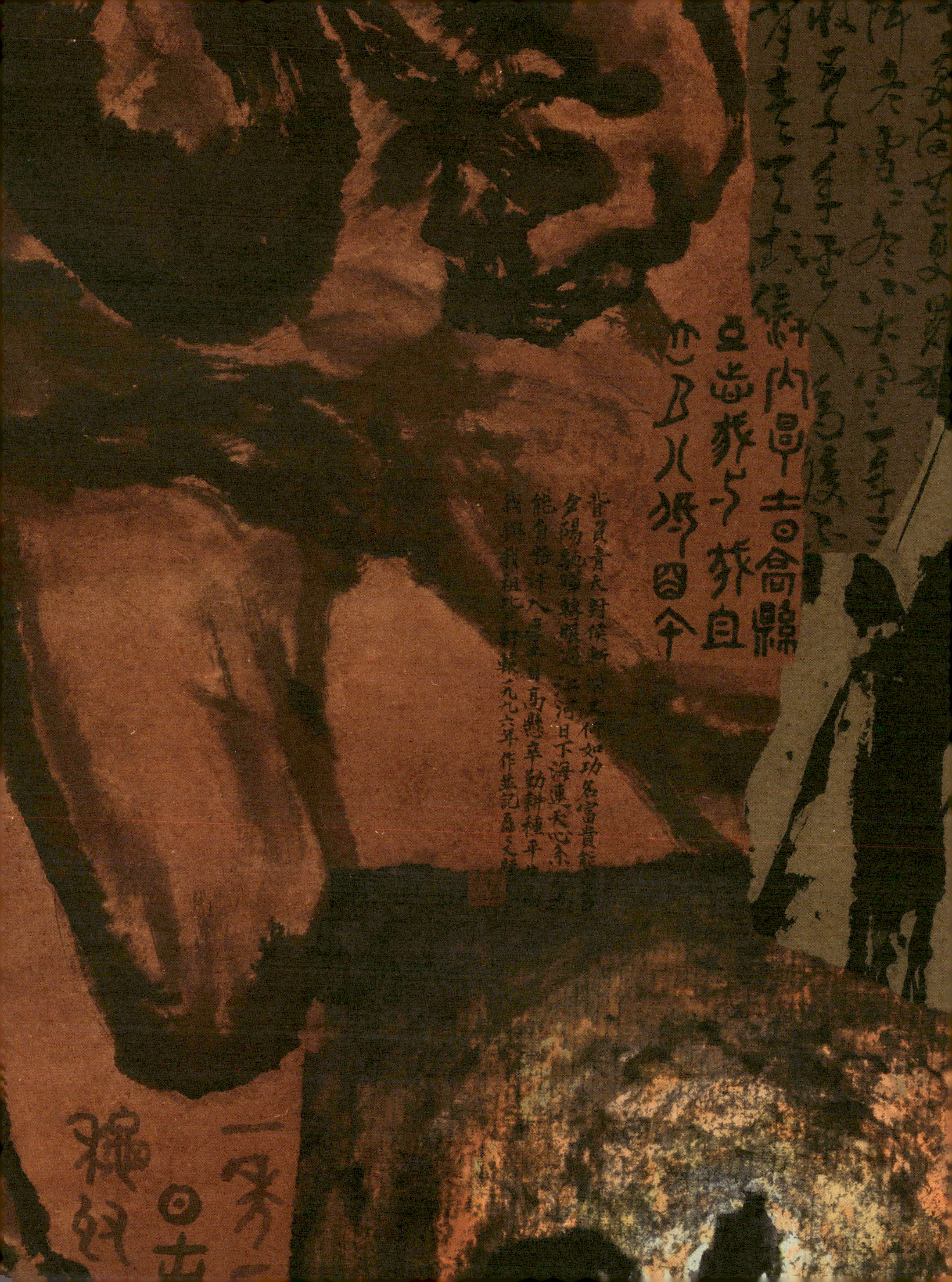

Qu Leilei
A Chinese Artist in Britain

Yan Liu

ASHMOLEAN

Acknowledgements

I wish firstly to add my thanks to those expressed by the Director of the Ashmolean in his Foreword to Jiangsu Art Reproduction & Culture Development Co. Ltd, and particularly to Mr Gao Lei, Mr Luo Qing, and Mrs Zhang Huaibing for their generous support of the exhibition catalogue. Within the Museum I am grateful to the Departments of Paper Conservation, Publications, Photo Studio, Exhibitions and Registrars, and to my colleagues in Eastern Art for all their kindness and help. Special thanks are due to Dr Alexander Sturgis, Professor Shelagh Vainker and Dr Mallica Kumbera Landrus for their support and continual encouragement, and Dr Rose Kerr for her wonderful essay. I would also like to thank Riad Nassar for the amazing filming, and Felicitas von Droste zu Hülshoff who is actively engaged in exhibition promotion and events programme planning. I also want to extend my gratitude to Dr Sarah Ng of Baptist University of Hong Kong for her valuable comments. Last, but not least, heartfelt thanks go to Qu Leilei and Caroline Deane for lending key works and their trust in pursuing this exhibition project.

Yan Liu
Christensen Fellow in Chinese Painting
Eastern Art Department
Ashmolean Museum of Art and Archaeology

Qu Leilei: A Chinese Artist in Britain
7 November 2017 to 15 April 2018

ISBN: 978-1-910807-20-0

British Library Cataloguing in Publication Data.
A catalogue record for this book is available from the British Library.

Designed by Ocky Murray
Printed and bound in Malta by Gutenberg Press

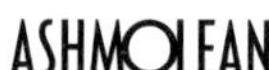

Contents

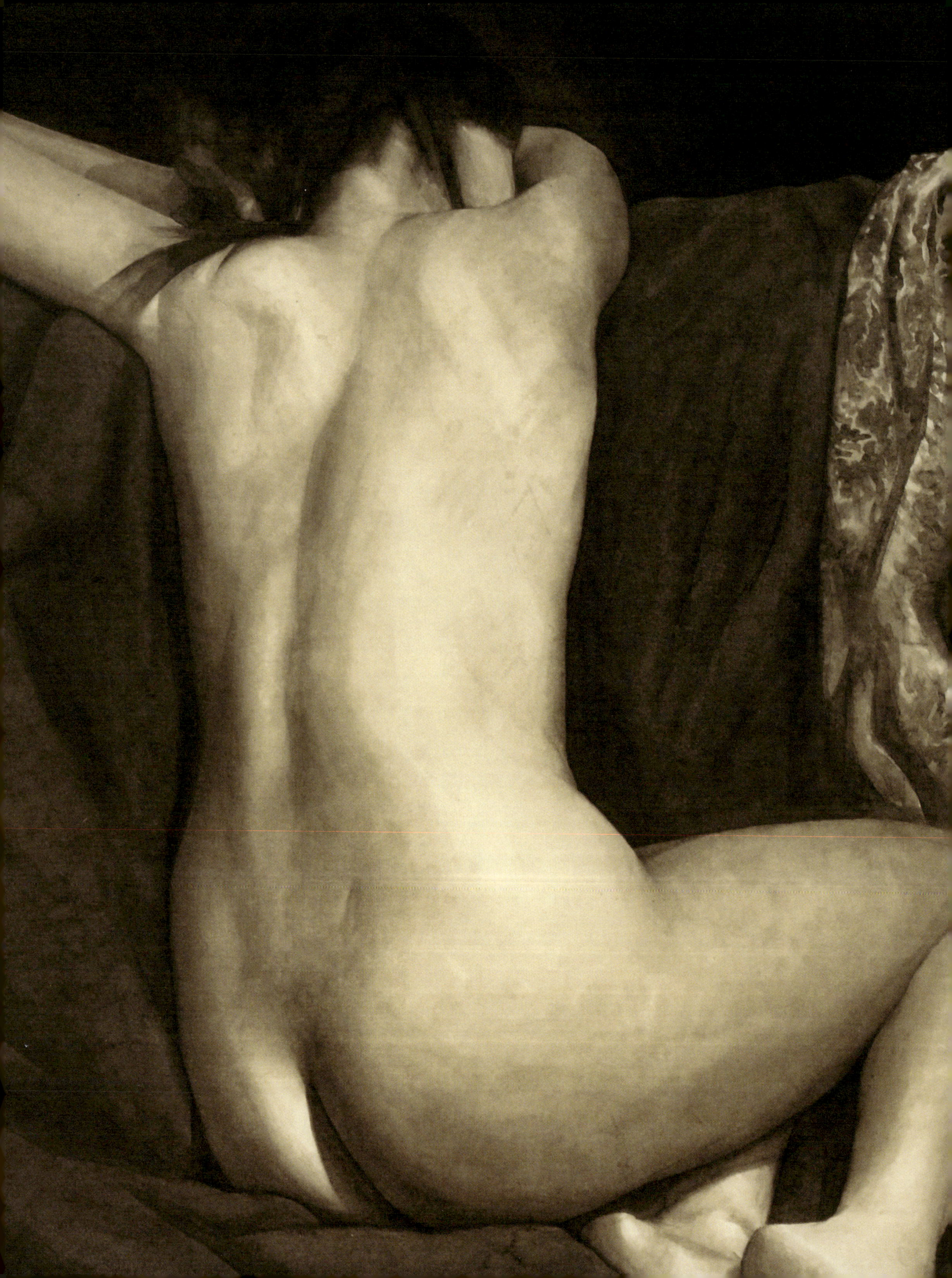

Director's Foreword

The Ashmolean Museum has been collecting modern and contemporary Chinese ink painting since the 1950s and thanks to significant gifts from the Reyes family in the 1990s and the transformative bequest from Professor Michael Sullivan in 2013 we now hold one of the most important collections of this material in the West.

Our programme of exhibitions in the Michael and Khoan Sullivan Gallery seeks to make this collection as accessible as possible while also drawing attention to the variety of work of contemporary Chinese artists working within or responding to the tradition of Chinese ink painting. This book accompanies the exhibition *Qu Leilei: a Chinese Artist in Britain*, the third in a series of monographic exhibitions we have mounted focussed on the work of major Chinese contemporary artists who have developed the techniques and aesthetics of Chinese ink painting in new and intriguing ways and follows those devoted to Xu Bing (2013) and Liu Dan (2016). Qu Leilei is a London-based Chinese artist whose large-scale works draw on both Eastern and Western traditions and techniques in a way that also speaks to the Ashmolean's abiding concern to explore the connections and influences that exist between different cultures.

We would particularly like to thank the Jiangsu Art Reproduction and Culture Development Co. Ltd for their generous support of the exhibition catalogue and above all to Qu Leilei and Caroline Deane for their collaboration and support in the development of this exhibition.

Alexander Sturgis
Director
Ashmolean Museum

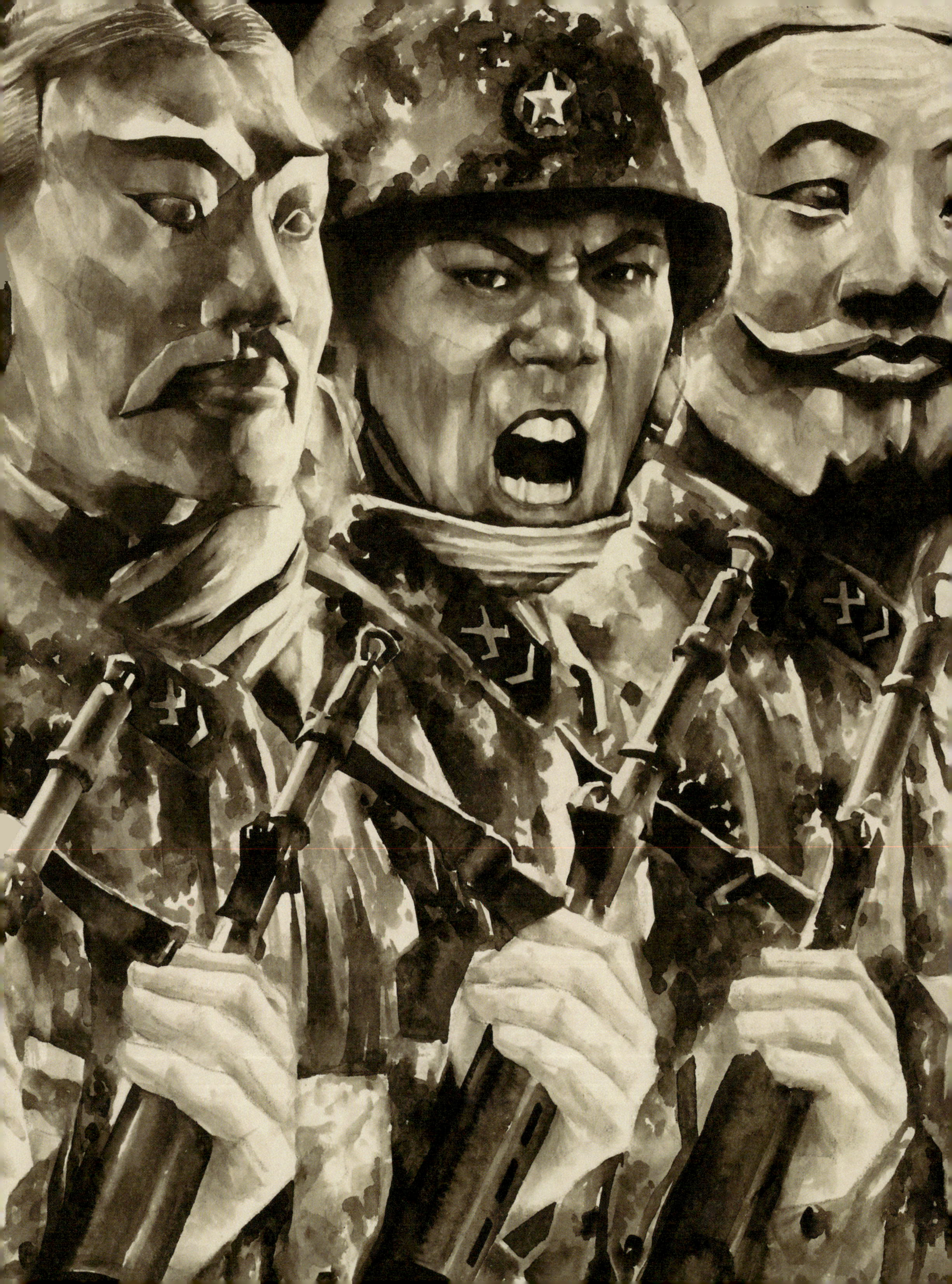

Preface
The way I see it
Qu Leilei

The evolution of my work and art may be broadly visualised as a journey consisting of three stages. When I was very young, even before my twenties, my focus amounted to a pure interest in art, combined with a fascination for drawing. Only later, when my situation permitted, did it develop into a career and the lifestyle that I know and love today. I have been fortunate to achieve this.

The real beginning for me was the 1979 'Stars Group', where I became immersed in a comparatively free, more liberal and creative environment. Surrounded by the stimulus of so many contemporary ideas, I started for the first time to really think about where I was going. Then the year 1989, a historical turning point with its dramatic events, provided another spark for me. Ultimately this was to lead to a deeper understanding of what kind of man I wanted to be, and what kind of art I wanted to create.

Over the last three decades, approximately every five years, I have concentrated upon a series of projects, each with a singular vision. I wanted them all to leave a footprint in their own way.

From 1985 to 1989, following my arrival in the UK, I produced my 'British Life' series of works. It reflected a basic desire to put down some roots in a new country. These paintings, at times slightly comical, were essentially a reaction to the 'humdrum chaos' of my everyday life in London at that time.

From 1990 to 1995 I concentrated upon the 'Sun in my Dream' series. These works sought to reflect and analyse half a lifetime of experience, and what I felt I had learned from this. Here my paintings ultimately symbolised my new awareness of the political environment that I found myself in.

From 1996 to 1999 I worked upon a series called 'Here and Now Facing the Future'. In this I set out to explore the concept of looking beyond myself, with an eye to expressing what we all have in common as human beings. I sought to explore what actually unites us with one another and to visualise humanity as a unified whole. In this series I wanted to show what links us as members of the same species, along with our ideals and hopes.

From 2000 to 2005 my focus was upon the 'Everyone's Life is an Epic' series. This project set out to research, express and highlight the poignancy of ordinary peoples' lives. My aim was to create an understanding of the underlying drama which we might have initially missed, or even dismissed as mundane.

My next series of works, spanning the years 2006 to 2010, was called 'Brush, Ink, Light, Shadow'. This aesthetic series celebrates the language of brush and ink in the light of a modern perspective, and seeks to merge artistic elements from the East and West.

From 2011 onwards I have been working on 'The Empire' series. Here I attempt to research, express and interpret aspects of Chinese history, acknowledging its ironies and responding to the questions that such analysis throws out at us. These works also consider how the disasters, pitfalls and tragedies that emerge from history are echoed in the present day.

As I look back over 30 years of research and experimentation, I can see a thread that unifies all my work. From concept, art form, media and technique, there lies within all the projects a deep concern for people's real living conditions. My art represents a search for a more profound understanding of life's value, the meaning it holds and the essential freedom and dignity of humanity.

Furthermore, my brush and ink artworks on xuan paper comprise explorations into the nature of light and shadow. From a Chinese Guo Hua (national painting) perspective, this actually represents a significant break with tradition. Although still in essence very Chinese, these images set out to embrace the Western aesthetic traditions, merging East and West as seamlessly as possible. The understanding of anatomy I acquired while holed up in Beijing Medical University during the Cultural Revolution has quite fortuitously given me a deep working knowledge of how the human body is composed.

People sometimes find my work hard to place in a certain category or 'ism'. Yet I am quite happy with this. I do not particularly want to belong to any specific movement or group, and do not find myself searching for one. I hope my work stands freely on its own. Its influences and directions reflect the times in my life, but also come from hours simply spent in the studio, seeing where inspiration will take me. These influences are neither Eastern or Western, but a combination of both. I hope and believe my paintings inspire and speak for themselves, with little need of justification.

The art of Qu Leilei
A series of natural and spontaneous changes

Rose Kerr

The great Daoist philosopher Laozi wrote:

Life is a series of natural and spontaneous changes. Don't resist them; that only creates sorrow. Let reality be reality. Let things flow forward naturally in whatever way they like.
致虛極，守靜篤。萬物並作，吾以觀複。夫物芸芸，各複歸其根。歸根曰靜，靜曰覆命。覆命曰常，知常曰明。不知常，妄作凶。知常容，容乃公，公乃全，全乃天，天乃道，道乃久，沒身不殆 。
(ch.16 第十六章)

These words seem to me to express the essence of Qu Leilei's art, which has constantly sought to renew itself while expressing life's realities. The range and richness of his work have reflected both personal and political concerns. Through the course of his career he has made changes in style and subject, and I have no doubt that new ideas and subjects will evolve for him in the future, their expression flowing forward in a natural way.

In the first part of his career Leilei, who had a thorough training in drawing, painting and calligraphy, used those skills on experimental work. In 1976 he employed line drawing for a series called 'World Famous Scientists', expressing his longing for China to modernise through science and democracy. The ending of the Cultural Revolution enabled thoughts and feelings prohibited for years to flow from the nib of his pen. He utilised papercuts and collages in such works as *Motherland* and *Enigma of an Ancient Country* and created oil paintings like *Filling up the Sea* and *Shooting the Sun*. Their titles are redolent of a struggle to understand the past and present of his troubled country. During this period Leilei worked for China Central Television, where he was involved with the excavation of the famous terracotta army. In 1981 he painted a series of oil paintings themed around the terracotta warriors including *Awakening* and *Descendants of the Dragon*; they acted as precursors to his recent work in the series 'A Thousand Years of Empire'. Over the next four years Leilei studied and experimented with twentieth-century Western art styles, in order to enrich his own work. He poured his thoughts into hundreds of visual diaries, posing relentless questions – *'Who am I, where am I from and where am I going to?'* – that found expression in drawings and collages. In 1985 he left China for the UK, thereby entering a new phase in his life and his career as an artist.

Leilei's early life in England was characterised by a wish to introduce Chinese ink painting to his new-found Western environment, while also allowing that foreign environment to influence and shape his own work. These ideas are exemplified in the brush paintings on 'English Life': a wry, affectionate series accompanied by humorous poems and captions. Studies of cathedrals, townscapes and landscapes are inescapably English, though painted in calligraphic Chinese inks. Leilei also undertook a number of painted and drawn nude studies, and spent considerable time in museums and art galleries scrutinising European masters. He studied to reconcile their achievements with his own experiences in Chinese painting.

This ruminative period was brought to an abrupt end by the events in Beijing of June 1989. Leilei dropped what he was working on to concentrate on more focused images. His work *Tian an Men 1989* proved a turning point in his art and in his life. It was followed by the series *The Sun in My Dream*, *The First Half of My Life* and other works such as *The Man's Tear*, *Between Sky and Earth*, *Just Wait*, *The Creator of Civilization*, *Carry the Sun to My Land* and *Here and Now*. As an expatriate Leilei was able to reflect on events in China in a savage and uncompromising manner. He began to incorporate various elements of painting, calligraphy, poetry, colour and collage into his style, describing this effort as a 'creative continuation' of the Chinese art tradition.

As the twentieth century drew to a close Qu Leilei started his 'Facing the New Century' series, attempting to express universal sentiment with all mankind. He came up with the idea of using simple pictures of the human hand that would transcend class, race and gender. Yet his paintings were more than straightforward visual images – they represented an urgent proclamation to humankind to confront the opportunities, challenges and crises of the world. Their technique was interesting because, despite appearing realistic in a Western style, they were in fact painted entirely in Chinese brush-and-ink. When exhibited in 1999 the paintings surrounded a central installation of ancient stones, collected from the British coastline and arranged so that their natural striations spelled out the message 'The whole of history appears in silence'.

The installation was completed by an audio track of breaking sea waves.

When the new century started Qu Leilei turned his whole energy towards the lives of ordinary people, believing that they reflected the value and dignity of humanity. His series 'Everyone's Life is an Epic' consists of paintings of Asian and European people from many walks of life, all of whom were active participants in the project. After talking with his subjects at length about their experiences, hopes and beliefs, Leilei completed each work by encouraging participants to write a message in their own hand on the finished piece. In 2005 the giant portraits were hung in the Ashmolean Museum, surrounding another stone installation that read 'Everyone's Life is an Epic' and accompanied by a soundtrack. This series is technically extremely competent, and it also indicates a fusion of East and West in subject matter and technique.

Around 2005 Leilei set a new challenge for himself. Still employing the traditional Chinese brush on xuan paper he set out to attain the effects of light, shadow and three-dimensional form achieved by European Renaissance painters. The subjects were a series of life-size nudes. The figures were anatomically correct, for Leilei had studied anatomy at Beijing Medical University, and their appearance was naturalistic, the ink following every contour of the body and gradation of the skin. I think it is true to say that no other ink painter has managed to capture modelling and chiaroscuro with such skill. The pictures are chiefly composed of black, grey and white. In Chinese terms these provide balancing tonalities of *yin* and *yang*; in Western terms they convey three-dimensionality through light and shade.

From 2010 onwards Qu Leilei worked on the project 'A Thousand Years of Empire'. The pictures depict warriors in the terracotta army merged with the image of Mao's hero, Lei Feng. Lei Feng was a soldier who became an icon of selfless and patriotic devotion to Party and country, his exploits used as a role model in both literature and art. The meaning behind the pictures was Leilei's realisation that 2000 years of Chinese history had not changed the position of the individual within society. Soldier figures ancient and modern served as single cogs within a highly organised system, sacrificing their lives for the needs of the State and the commands of a despotic ruler. In a more recent work, *Soldiers*, the artist's intention was to encompass a broader, international perspective. Warfare is a recurring scar on world history, from the battles of Qin Shihuangdi in the third century BC to contemporary struggles in Syria and Iraq.

The present exhibition at the Ashmolean Museum is a retrospective, a view of the body of work Qu Leilei has produced up to the present day. Certain broad themes can be divined: a compelling interest in the history of China, and what can be learned from it; a loving concern for human beings and their individual achievements; an absorption in the anatomy and depiction of the human body; a powerful urge to warn against the perils of the world; and a heartfelt desire to integrate Chinese and Western art practice and techniques. Those themes have been pursued with ever-increasing skill down the years. Qu Leilei now stands as a technically accomplished master, capable of handling brush and ink with the utmost competence. His visual language is well established, and it represents a fusion of East and West.

Some ink painters have chosen to push boundaries by making traditional styles more abstract or ornamented. By contrast Leilei has sought to blend descriptive, realistic styles of the European Renaissance with Chinese ink painting. Moreover, he has constantly worked to achieve profound concepts in his work, ideas that have universal application. Such goals have not been achieved with ease. As Leilei himself has observed:

It is easier to talk about events, and even to an extent to write about them. But to paint pictures about them was and is not easy. I only wanted to show what I thought, as clearly as possible and with as much integrity as I could find. This is only my interpretation of the world and I want to take other peoples' views into account, so that I can learn more.

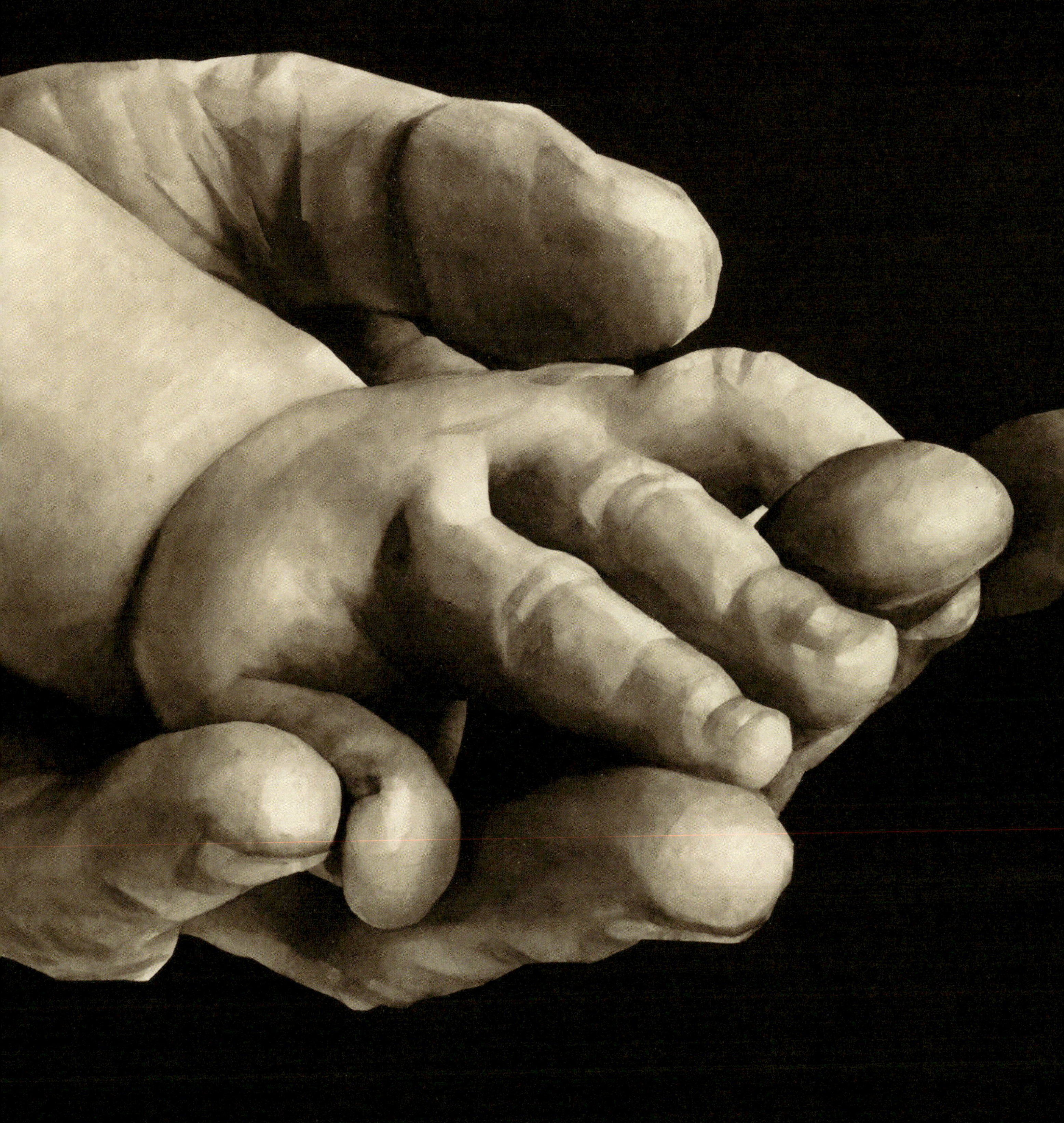

Introduction

Qu Leilei 曲磊磊 (b.1951) is an international artist based in London. He was born and bred in the political and cultural turbulence of late twentieth-century China. He started his career as a founding member of the famous avant-garde 'Stars Group' in China before moving to England to study Western Art in 1985. His work has been exhibited in galleries and museums in China, Hong Kong and the UK for over 30 years and is represented in a large number of private collections around the world. Qu Leilei's innovative contribution to ink art is well-established in his monochrome figural painting, the primary focus of this exhibition. This genre of art represents his distinctive visual language, blending lively brushwork and Western technique with sensitivity and virtuosity. Many of his paintings explore the ways in which a Chinese artist works with ink on paper to express his experience as an immigrant and to preserve the memory of his earlier life. Unlike many of his contemporaries, the artist's particular gift is his ability to unite East and West, tradition and contemporaneity, past and present. The significance of his art lies in the complex interplay of aesthetics, immigrant experience and Chinese history.

Modern Chinese ink painting: historical background

'Modern Chinese ink painting' is a term now commonly employed by artists and critics, but conceptual ambiguity still surrounds its use. On one hand, 'Chinese ink painting' often applies to any artwork painted in ink on rice paper. For centuries the Chinese aesthetic of brush and ink has been appreciated for its deep and fascinating roots in painting and calligraphy. Chinese ink painting was described by the scholars of twentieth-century China as *guohua*, literally meaning 'national painting', which was used to distinguish Chinese paintings executed in traditional media from works that employed Western methods and materials, such as oil on canvas.[1] There can be no doubt that ink painting and calligraphy, considered to be the core of Chinese art, could not have survived in the twentieth century without modern nationalism.[2] On the other hand the term 'modern Chinese ink painting' refers to a type of painting that imbues the spirit of traditional ink art with elements of Western art.[3] In the early decades of the century creative artists searched for inspiration from the West, devoting themselves to promoting and transforming Chinese ink painting. The Lingnan School (active 1906–51) attempted to create a new style of ink painting, originally inspired by study in late Meiji Japan, but its works reflect an indirect Western influence.[4]

It was only after the Second World War that Chinese artists began to travel more frequently to Europe. For example, in 1946 the British Council sent Zhang Anzhi 張安治 (1911–90), Chen Xiaonan 陳曉南 (1908–93), Zhang Qianying 張蒨英 (1909–2003) and Fei Chengwu 費成武 (1911–2000), all then working with Xu Beihong 徐悲鴻 (1895–1953) in Nanjiang, to study in London.[5] In 1947 Wu Guanzhong 吳冠中 (1919–2010) travelled to Paris to study European painting; he subsequently turned to a traditional medium and worked with ink on paper in the 1970s. Zhao Wuji 趙無極 (1921–2013) arrived in Paris in 1948. Here he developed an individual style influenced by European abstraction, preferring to work with oil paints in a calligraphic style. In 1972 Zhao abandoned colour and painted only in monochrome ink. His paintings take on the form of abstract expressionism and embody the essence of Chinese aesthetics.

The modern art movement initiated by a group of artists in the 1960s was one of the most decisive reforms of modern Chinese ink painting. The group introduced new themes, techniques and ideas to Chinese painting, at the same time serving to reaffirm the strength and vitality of the tradition itself. The artists also sought to establish their own cultural identity.[6] The group included Taiwanese painters Liu Guosong 劉國松 (b.1932),

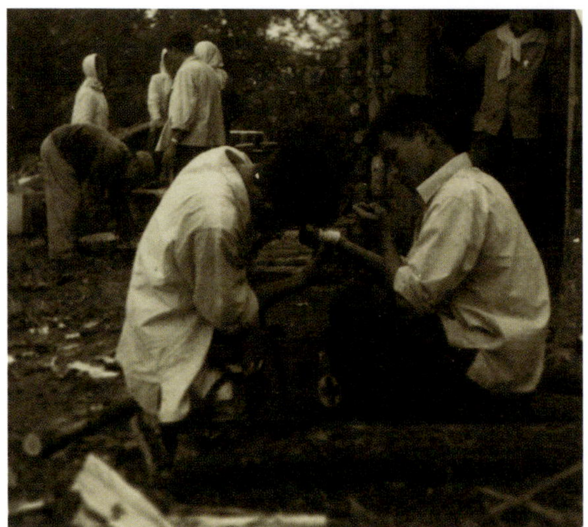

Fig.1 Qu Leilei attending to a patient, 1968. He worked as a 'barefoot doctor' during the Cultural Revolution. Photo courtesy of Qu Leilei

Fig.2 Qu Leilei, *Facing the Sun*, 1987. Collage

Fig.3 Qu Leilei, *Fisted Hands*, 1983. Ink and colour on paper

who encountered American abstract expressionism when he went to the US in 1966, and Feng Zhongrui 馮鐘睿 (b.1933), who studied theatre design at the University of Hawaii in 1970. They used acrylic, ink and collage to create diverse images, borrowing the concepts of abstract expressionism to revitalise traditional ink painting. The Hong Kong artists, such as Lü Shoukun 呂壽琨 (1919–75), the leading painter in modern ink painting, and his followers, among them Wang Wuxie 王無邪 (b.1936), began exploring new ways to blend Western modernism and Chinese tradition. These stylistically diverse paintings illustrate a variety of new ink language.

The 1980s witnessed a vibrant cultural movement and a new wave of emigration. After the restrictions of the Cultural Revolution, China opened up to the outside world. Many Chinese artists went abroad to America and Europe to study Western art for inspiration. Others, well established in China, found it necessary to seek new audiences for their work in the West.[7] The development of multi-dimensional ink painting has evidently acquired more attention due to the impetus generated by new art methodologies. Artists such as Liu Dan 劉丹 (b.1953), Xu Bing 徐冰 (b.1955) and Gu Wenda 谷文達 (b.1955) boldly merge traditional and Western concepts, bringing many new elements to ink art. In varying degrees these artists adapted their work to the taste of their new audiences, taking new inspiration from art they found abroad.

Since 1990 an increasingly active dialogue has taken place between the Chinese and the global art market, raising the profile of ink painting created by diasporic artists. In 1998 'Inside Out: New Chinese Art', the first major exhibition assembled by the Asian Society Galleries in New York and the San Francisco Museum of Modern Art, presented artworks in a variety of media, including ink paintings, oils, installation and performance art. These were produced by artists in mainland China, Taiwan and Hong Kong, and also by Chinese artists who had migrated to the West since the late 1980s.[8] The exhibition marked an important showcase for diaspora Chinese artists in the United States.

In 2009 another exhibition, 'Outside In: Chinese x American x Contemporary Art', displayed Chinese contemporary art in the United States. Once again it affirmed the inventiveness of immigrant Chinese artists, providing fresh reflections on Chinese art and culture in their contemporary artistic expressions.[9]Among the various art forms, ink art, which sought to highlight the unique ways in which Chinese traditional art forms provide inspiration for contemporary artists, has evoked the most interest, gaining prominence worldwide. In 2013 the Metropolitan Museum of Art mounted its first major exhibition of contemporary Chinese ink art. It considered the work of contemporary Chinese artists who radically altered an inherited Chinese tradition while maintaining an underlying association with the expressive cultural language of the past.[10]

Expatriate Chinese artists have played a crucial role in defining Chinese art to audiences outside China, especially for Chinese ink painting which has previously received much less recognition in the West than Chinese oil painting or so-called avant-garde art. Most expatriate Chinese artists experimented with a non-traditional application of ink and colour in their reactions to the contemporary world. What separated overseas artists from those remaining in the country was not just geographical distance and cultural context, but also artistic ideals and personal experience – both reflected in their artistic background and activity.[11] Each artist responded differently to their physical displacement.[12] The ink art of Qu Leilei represents a unique and interesting example of how an individual artist with an immigrant origin investigates his cultural identity in the new country.

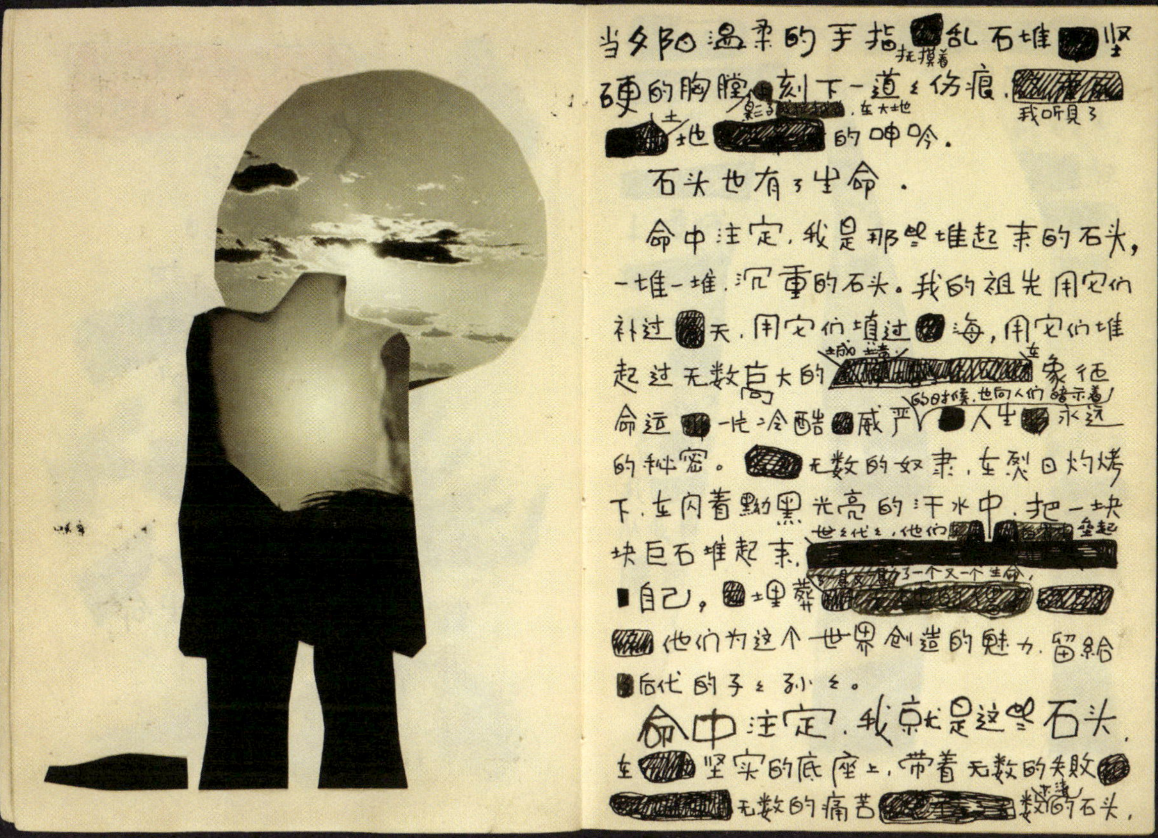

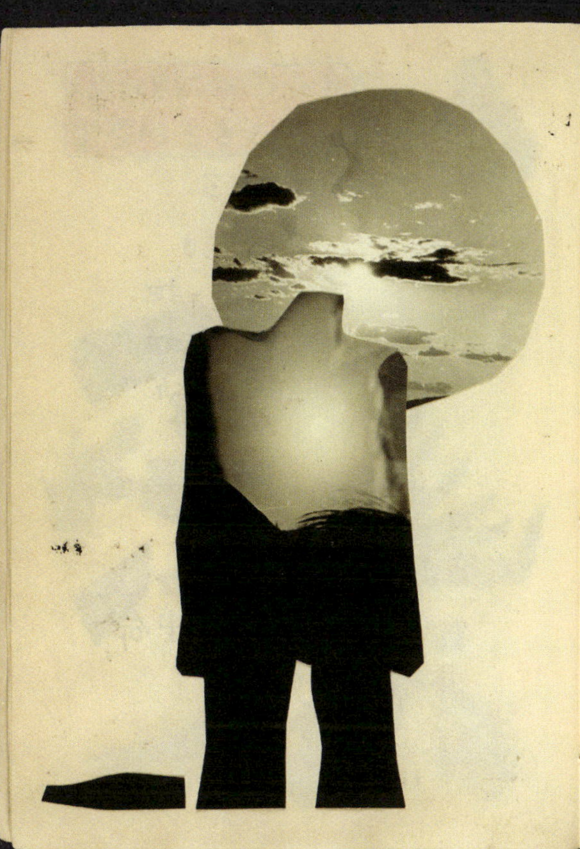

当夕阳温柔的手指乱石堆坚
硬的胸膛刻下一道道伤痕.
地的呻吟.
石头也有了生命.
命中注定,我是那些堆起来的石头,
一堆一堆,沉重的石头。我的祖先用它们
补过天,用它们填过海,用它们堆
起过无数高大的象征
命运一片冷酷威严人生永远
的秘密。无数的奴隶,在烈日灼烤
下,在闪着黝黑光亮的汗水中,把一块
块巨石堆起来,
自己,埋葬
他们为这个世界创造的魅力,留给
后代的子子孙孙。
命中注定,我就是这些石头,
在坚实的底座上,带着无数的失败
无数的痛苦数的石头,

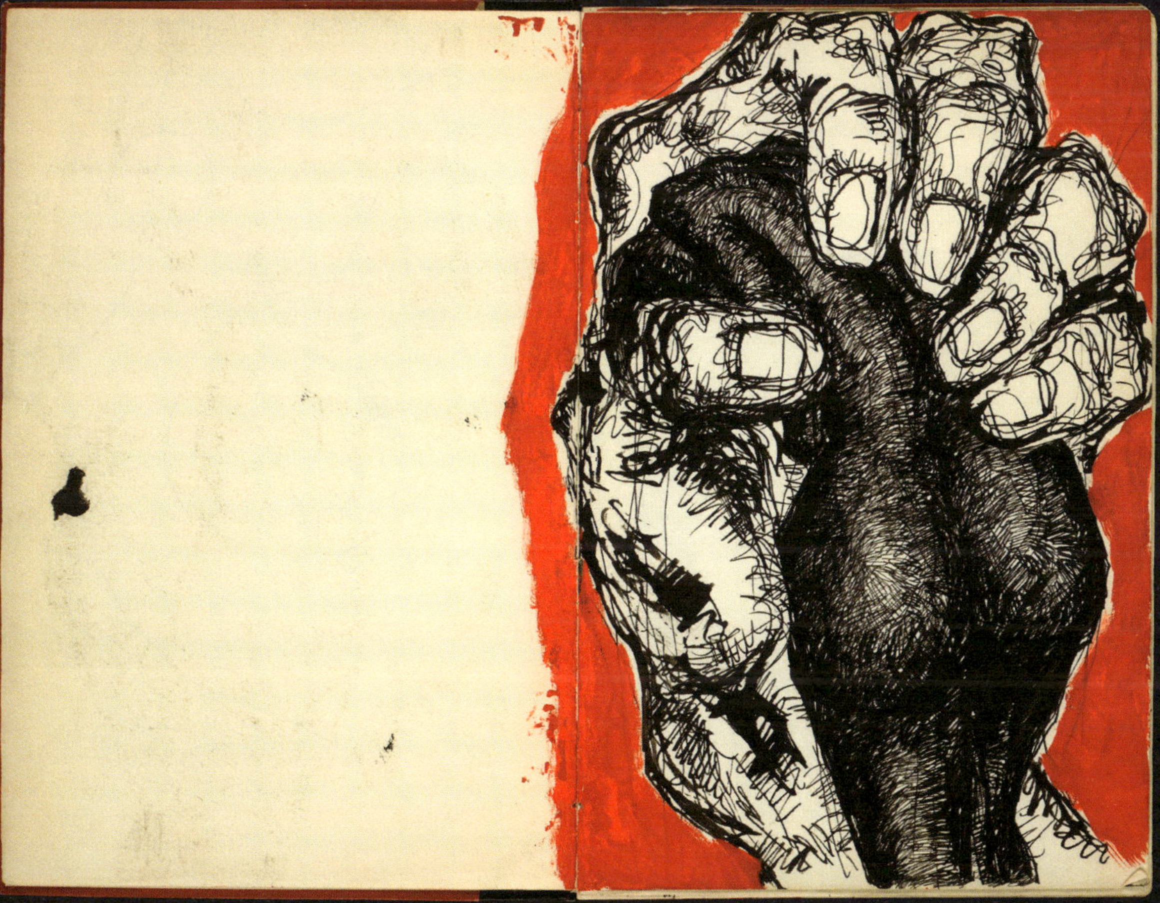

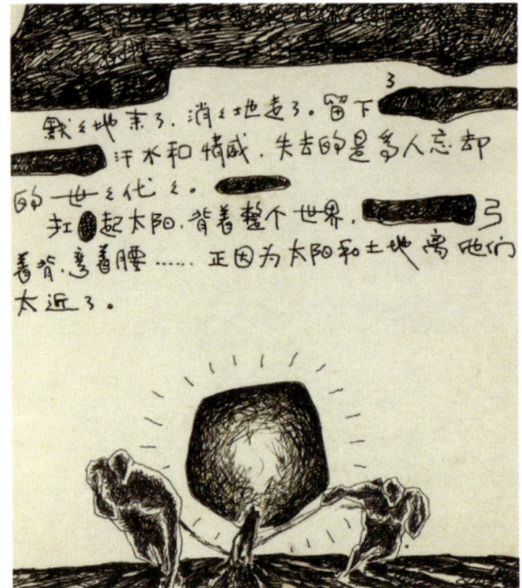

4

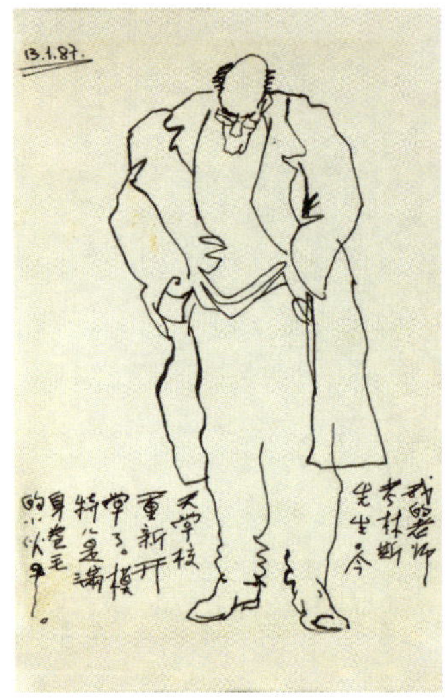

5

Fig.4 Qu Leilei, *Figures*, 1983. Ink on paper

Fig.5 Qu Leilei, *Cecil Collins*, 1987. Ink on paper

Ink art today is more pluralistic, and it is not restricted by subject, technique or style. Chinese ink painting has become a fertile area for experimentation and innovation, and various forms of modern and postmodern art from abroad have been introduced. Qu Leilei is an outstanding representative of the new trends of Chinese ink painting. The exhibition showcases a variety of images ranging from small sketches of life drawing to larger, highly refined figure paintings created from 1985 to the present, showing his progression from calligraphic collage to an exploration of a new vocabulary of ink language. This essay identifies some of Qu Leilei's sources and inspirations for his art and tracing the development of his personal style through artworks selected from the Ashmolean Museum and the artist's collection. These works fall into three main categories: calligraphic collage, abstract ink and figural painting.

Education and early career

Qu Leilei was born in an intellectual family in the northeastern province of Heilongjiang in 1951, the son of loyal communists who joined the Sino-Japanese War in 1938. His father Qu Bo曲波 (1923–2002) was a well-known writer, author of *Tracks in the Snowy Forest* 林海雪原 (*Linhai xueyuan*), which promoted communist counterinsurgency against remnants of nationalist armies in the late 1940s. His grandfather Qu Chunyang 曲春陽, the leader of a peasant army, died in a battle against the Beiyang warlord Zhang Zongchang 張宗昌 (1881–1932). Qu Leilei soon showed a strong interest in art. At the age of six he studied traditional Chinese painting and calligraphy under the private tutor Tan Wancun 譚萬村, a pupil of Qi Baishi 齊白石 (1864–1957). His education began with the traditional Chinese painting from the celebrated *Mustard Seed Garden Manual of Painting* 芥子園畫譜 (*Jieziyuan huapu*), first published between 1679 and 1701, which discusses artistic principles and methods and illustrates the way various subjects should be treated. This manual has been reprinted many times, and is still widely used to introduce beginners and new practitioners to ink painting.

Qu Leilei had the privilege of being introduced to Chinese painting through his father's friends in the Beijing circle of art and literature at an early age, including Yang Zhaohe 蔣兆和 (1904–86), Hua Junwu 華君武 (1915–2010), Yandi 顏地 (1920–79), Huang Yongyu 黃永玉 (b.1924), Huang Zhou 黃胄 (1925–97) and Sun Zixi 孫滋溪 (b.1929). Among these prominent artists, Huang Zhou was a frequent visitor, well known for his figure painting. He commented that the 14-year-old was a talented artist when he saw his drawings. He also told Qu Leilei some interesting stories about Chinese masters such as Qi Baishi, who often rotated the brush between his fingers when painting shrimps. In a creative process known as 'painting and calligraphy being of the same origin', the elasticity of brushes, delicate layers of ink and gentle texture and diffusion properties of xuan paper are important for excellent expression in ink painting. The directional change as the artist turned his wrist would create a sharper, more incisive line. Like other skilful painters Qi Baishi often kept using the central tip (*zhongfeng* 中鋒) of the brush, which creates a full and rounded line, rather than the side of the brush (*cefeng* 側鋒) for broader and angular strokes.[13]

When the Cultural Revolution reached his school in 1966, Qu Leilei was only 15. Deprived of a normal education, he taught himself painting and literature through books in his family's library. He also met some more artist friends of his father and studied painting with them. Qu Leilei's mastery of brush and ink, and profound knowledge of archaic Chinese scripts, benefitted from his earlier training in calligraphy. Like millions of other young people in China, he participated in producing propaganda art, including paintings of Chairman Mao. However, none of his paintings from the Cultural Revolution

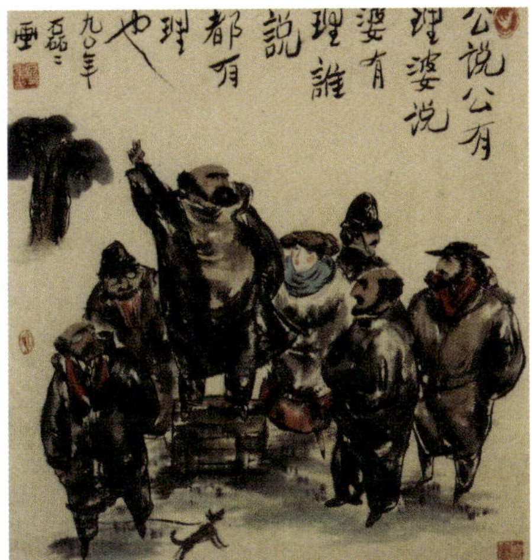

6

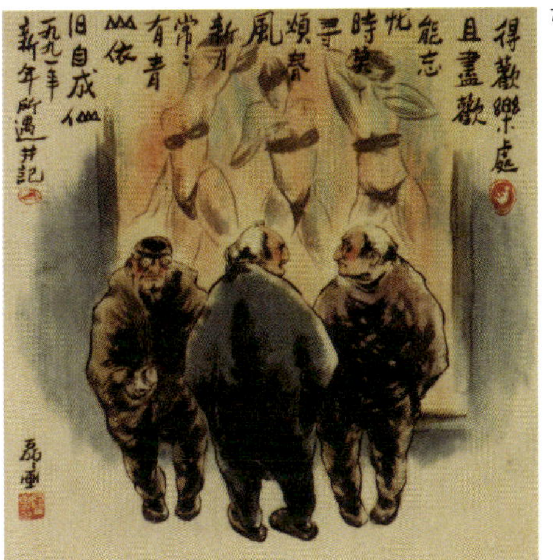

7

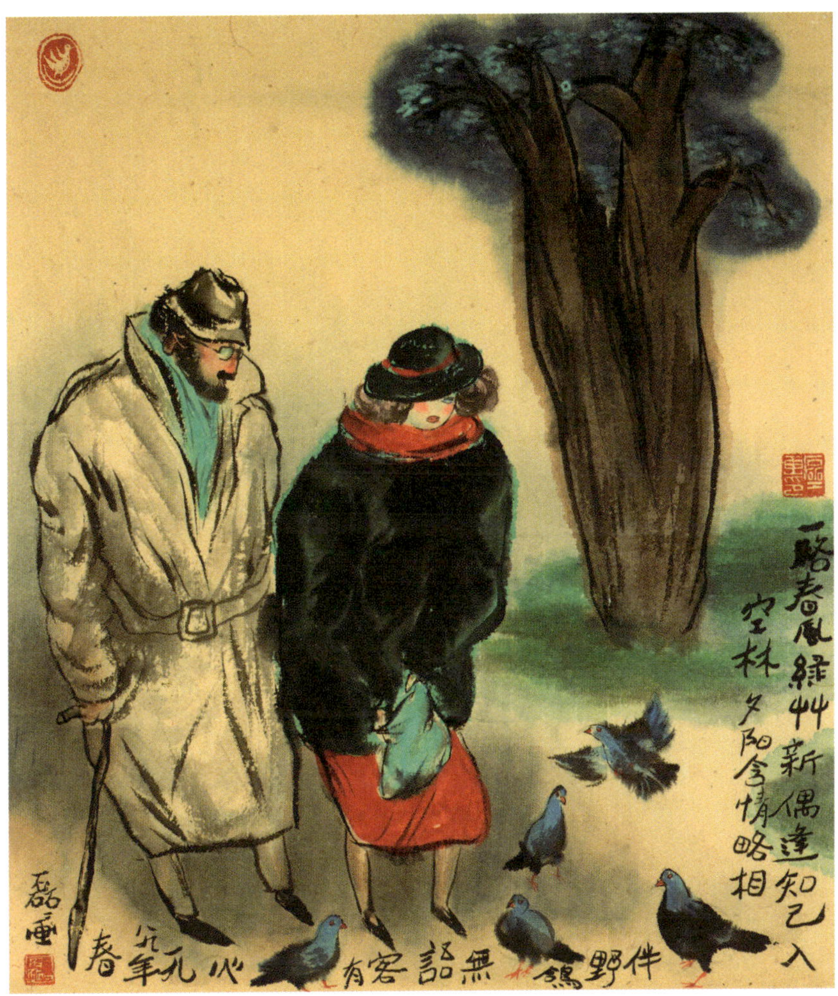

8

Fig.6 Qu Leilei, *Life in Britain: speaker at Hyde Park*, 1990. Ink and colour on paper

Fig.7 Qu Leilei, *Life in Britain: a group of gentlemen eyeing up bikini models*, 1991. Ink and colour on paper

Fig.8 Qu Leilei, *Life in Britain: a young couple*, 1989. Ink and colour on paper

era have survived. In 1968 Qu Leilei's parents were branded 'capitalists' and he was exiled to northeast China. Here he worked in the countryside as a peasant and a 'barefoot doctor' (Fig.1).[14] In 1969 he was enrolled in the army, and subsequently served as both a worker and an artist. In 1976 he studied human anatomy (including witnessing dissections of muscles) in Beijing Medical University, acquiring a deep understanding of anatomy. He later applied this knowledge to life-like portrayals of the human body in figural paintings.

The 'Stars' period

Chinese painting in 1980s sought a decisive break with the Maoist conceptual approaches that had dominated Chinese art since the 1960s. Politically these years saw the abdication of Deng Xiaoping (1904–97) and increased contact with the West. Artistically this period witnessed a wave of activity encouraging individualism and freedom of expression in the country. This was not entirely new, however. In 1976, after the death of Chairman Mao and the end of the Cultural Revolution, Qu Leilei had become a leading member of the 'Stars Group'星星 (*Xingxing*) – a Beijing-based group of 23 artists who campaigned passionately for greater freedom within the arts. Qu Leilei still sees himself as an advocate for this today. He seeks both to grasp the historical past and investigate the self-conscious creation of art within a context of tremendous economic and social change and the cultural conflicts that result.

During the 'Stars' period (1978–84), Qu Leilei expressed his thoughts and feelings about the nation's fate. He explored the historical mission of an individual artist – *Who am I, where am I from and where am I going to?* – in his drawings and collages. These works set out to express his inner feelings and his views on China's future.[15] This process of reflection led the artist to discover what was important in his own experience, and how this related to modern Chinese history. A few sketches from the 'Stars Group' era (Figs 2–4) reflect his predisposition for the creative use of collage technique and strong interest in the sculptural effect of human figures. Both thus date from long before his arrival in Britain.

Qu Leilei wrote a lot about the political trauma of the time, and the social changes that the nation had experienced. Both a personal and political past are deeply interwoven in his drawings. As a highly individualistic artist who saw much suffering in the Cultural Revolution, he expressed his emotions and understanding of the cost such a catastrophe has had on Chinese society. His drawings of this time powerfully convey the devastation: complete destruction of traditional cultures, values and belief systems, the physical torture of intellectuals, the disintegration of families, the collapse of the educational system and the exile of millions of young

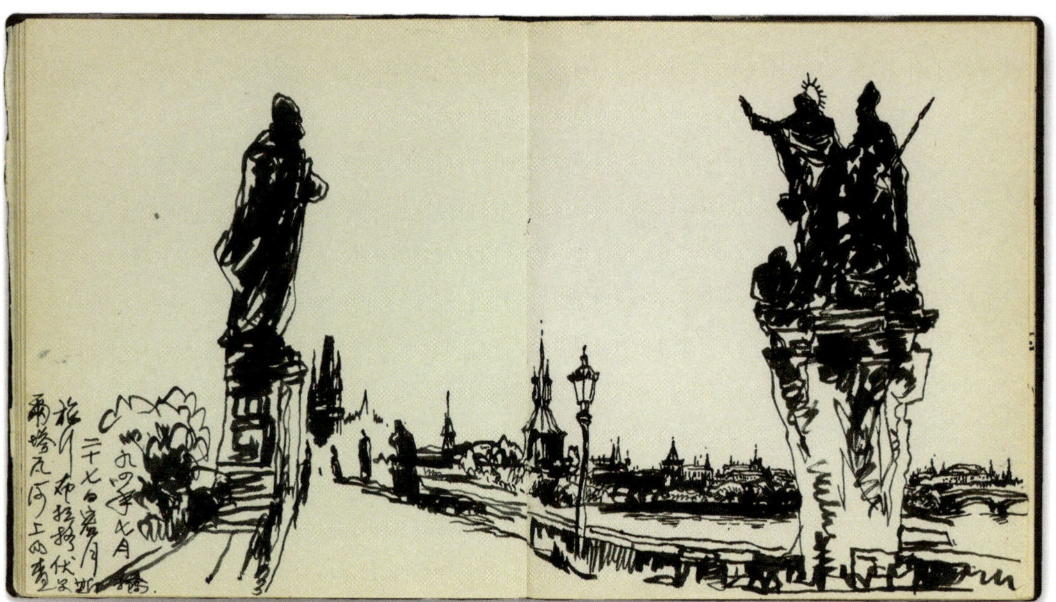

9

Fig.9 Qu Leilei, *The Charles Bridge at Prague*, 1994. Ink on paper

people to the countryside. The series of sketches titled as 'Brief Recollections' shows images of the death, violence and torture wrought by the Cultural Revolution. Qu Leilei declares that he grew up in an age with no moral standards or social rules.

Life in Britain

In 1985 Qu Leilei moved to Britain, part of the first wave of culturally conscious migrants in Chinese history.[16] From 1986 to 1987 he studied Western art at the Central College of Art in London under Cecil Collins (1908–89). Cecil Collins has been recognised as belonging to the Neo-Romantic movement of poetical art which flourished in the post-war period, but his dedication to depicting a mystical understanding made his work highly distinctive.[17] Through emblematic figures such as the Fool, the Angel, the Pilgrim and the Sibyl in extraordinary landscapes, Collins portrayed an original and inspiring philosophy of life. From his study with Collins (Fig.5), Qu Leilei was able to learn how to 'abandon control' through the process of life drawing.

Fascinated by the different culture and people in Britain, Qu Leilei painted a remarkable series of sketches of English life in the 1990s. He captured in a very graphic style the simple beauty of everyday life that he saw while living in London. Travellers on the Tube, the advocate at Speaker's Corner in Hyde Park, a group of gentlemen eyeing up bikini-clad models, a couple strolling down a garden path (Figs 6–8) became the major subjects of his art. In 1994 he married Caroline Deane. She is a British artist who studied oil painting in England before attending the Central Academy of Fine Arts in Beijing as a visiting graduate student in 1989. In 1994 the couple visited Prague on honeymoon, exploring the Charles Bridge (Fig.9), the Vltava River and the Old Town Square in this picturesque city. In 1996 their daughter Taotao was born. Qu Leilei made numerous sketches of her, one of which shows Taotao aged three, seated with Caroline in Wimbledon Park (Fig.10).

An ancient Chinese proverb runs 'Walk ten thousand miles, read ten thousand books'. Travel is seen as an integral part of artists' aesthetic experience, an opportunity for different kinds of landscapes to refresh their creative drive. As he travelled around the world with his family, Qu Leilei made a large number of watercolour sketches, from Zulu warriors at the Shakaland Cultural Village in South Africa (Fig.11) to the historical city of Bergen in Norway (Fig.12). He maintains an interest in empirical research, sketching from nature and people he has seen. His sketchbooks of landscape and people on display reveal the impact of overseas experience on the development of Qu Leilei's individual style. Discovering different climates, natural landscapes, architecture, people and culture, and encountering things new or unknown all proved sources of artistic inspiration, investing his creativity with a rich new visual vocabulary.

Qu Leilei has also remained in constant touch with China. His more distant perspective allows him to view cultural and aesthetic traditions more objectively and to engage with them more freely. This rich combination of influences and stimuli – Chinese tradition, Western art and overseas experience – produced the ideal conditions to nurture his talent. As he became more established in Britain Qu Leilei began to create his own formal language, founded on the study of calligraphic collage with Chinese ink and colour.

Calligraphic collage

Collage comes from the French word '*coller*' (to glue), and 'collage' thus means 'a glued work'. As a new artistic medium, collage became hugely influential after the birth of cubism, when it was occasionally used by Picasso and Braque for artistic innovation.[18] The medium was favoured by many

Fig.10 Qu Leilei, *Caroline Deane and Taotao at Wimbledon Park*, 1999. Ink on paper

Fig.11 Qu Leilei, *Zulu Warriors of the Shakaland Cultural Village, South Africa*, 2009. Ink and watercolour on paper

Fig.12 Qu Leilei, *Bergen, Norway*, 2012. Watercolour on paper

10

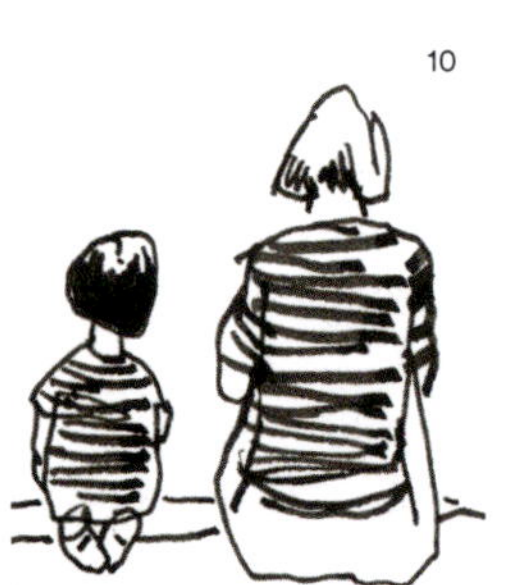

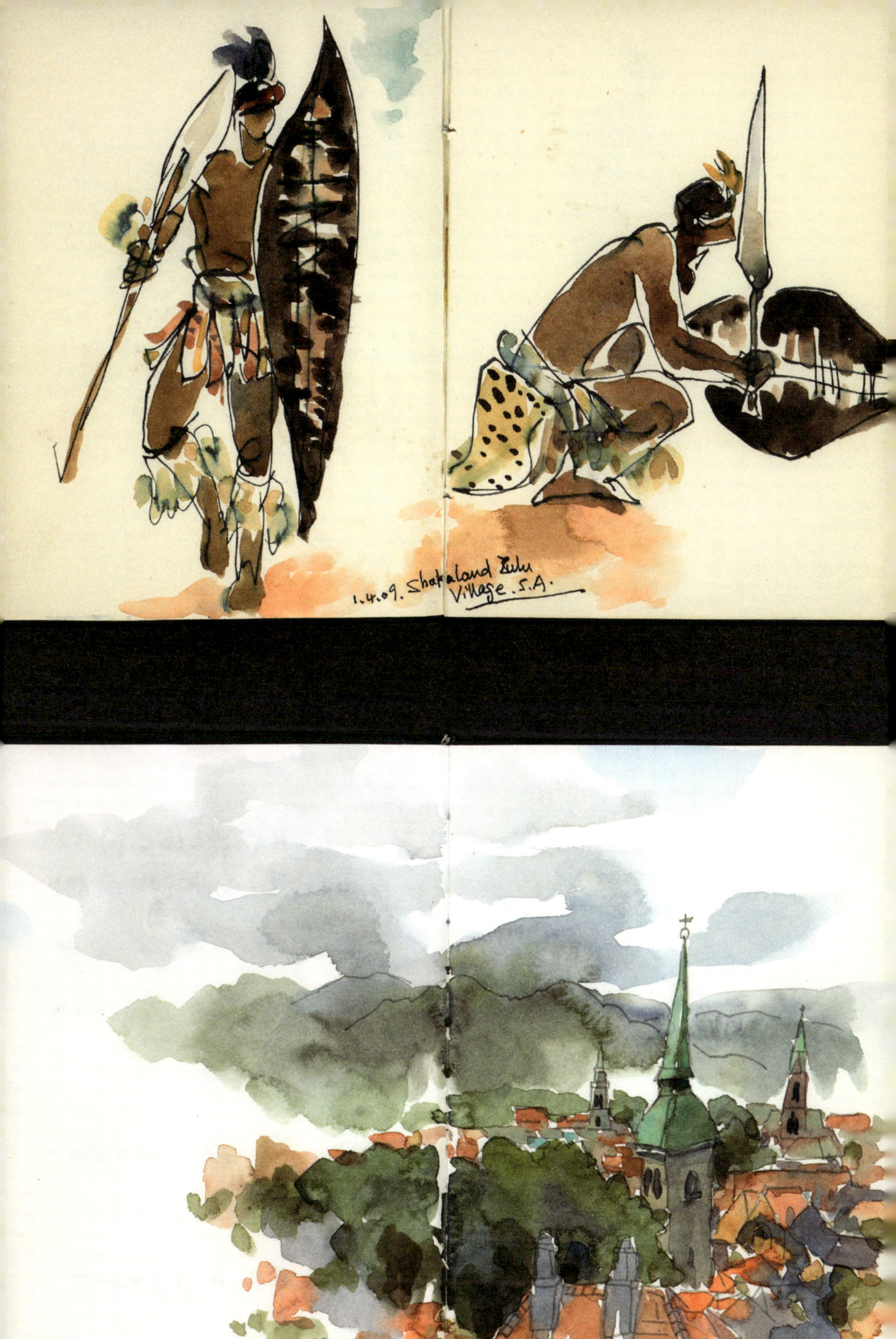
1.4.09. Shakaland Zulu
Village. S.A.
8.7.12.
Bergen
Norway.

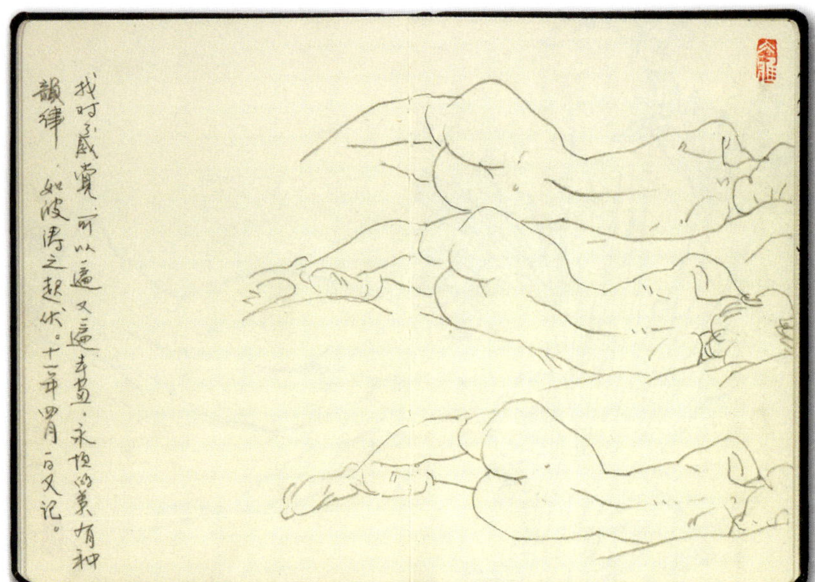

Fig.13 Qu Leilei, *Nude study*, May 2011. Pencil on paper

artists from modernism to the present day, especially to create images of ambiguity.

Using collage for ink art is not entirely new for Chinese artists. Since 1960 leading artists from the Fifth Moon Group have used oils, acrylic, collage and Chinese ink to create a new style of Chinese painting, responding to the challenge of Western modernism. Liu Guosong 劉國松 (b.1932) adopted the materials of ink painting and began experimenting with collage, ink rubbing and free brushwork to create abstract landscapes with bold, expressionist brushstrokes.[19] Zhuang Zhe 莊哲 (b.1934), who moved to New York in 1973, worked on oils and acrylic on canvas, reflecting the abstract expressionist influence of time spent in Europe and the United States. In 1989 Fong Zhongrui 馮鐘睿 (b.1933) applied acrylic onto thin sheets of plastic to produce unpredictable patterns, transferred in turn on to papers or canvas.[20]

Qu Leilei began experimenting with collage and ink on paper almost at the same time as the Fifth Moon Group painters. However, his collage can be distinguished in two main ways. First, calligraphy is predominant in his images. Usually there are no decipherable Chinese characters in the works of the Fifth Moon School artists, which have become closer to abstract painting than to calligraphy. By contrast Qu Leilei's work uses a variety of archaic scripts for their formal beauty and elegance, in addition to their literal and symbolic meanings. Second, he developed a new form of collage with ink on paper. The rich texture and different tones of his work are indebted to the traditional techniques used for mounting Chinese scrolls.

The Creator of Civilization (Cat.1) unites words and images to create a social commentary on the fate of the nation and Chinese history. Farming was a recurring theme in many Chinese historical paintings, but this image of men toiling in the fields is imbued with the memories of stress, pain, hardship and endurance. The powerful male figure, depicted with bold brushwork, represents the artist himself, who laboured on a state farm during the Cultural Revolution. The collage is inscribed with different styles of texts, including small script, running script and standard script.[21] The major inscription reads 'The sage's only focus is the belly and not the eyes' '聖人為腹不為目', a quote from *The Classic of the Dao and Virtue* 道德经 (*Daodejing*) of Laozi (605–531 BC), an ancient Chinese philosopher and writer. A 112-character Chinese poem composed by the artist, depicting the agricultural theme, underpinned the foundation of modern civilisation.

春雨驚春請穀天	聖人為腹不為目	心系天地能自悟
夏滿芒夏暑相連	面向黃土背青天	汗入厚土日高懸
秋處露秋寒霜降	封侯斬將又何如	辛勤耕種平生志
冬雪雪冬小大寒	功名富貴能幾番	我與我祖皆軒轅
一年三百六十日	夕陽馳暉轉眼過	
春種秋收五千年	江河日下海連天	

This collage contains elements substantially similar to one of Qu Leilei's earlier works created in the 'Stars' period. The reclining male figure is executed with freehand brushwork in an abstract style. His image, interestingly, mirrors the one beneath the calligraphic brushstroke: a group of farmers are preparing the ground for cultivation. The gleaming light from the darkness, layered by a mixture of rich warm brown, orange and yellow tones, draws the viewer into an earlier age of fires and ploughs.

In some of Qu Leilei's collage works (Cats 2–4 and 6), the calligraphy can be poems from ancient times or excerpts from Buddhist *sutras*, composed by different scripts in ink and brush for aesthetic effect. Here the combination of images and text does not necessarily require the viewer to understand all the complex relationships and meanings. In *Where Are You Going To?* (Cat.5), Qu Leilei has borrowed some visual elements from Chinese history and

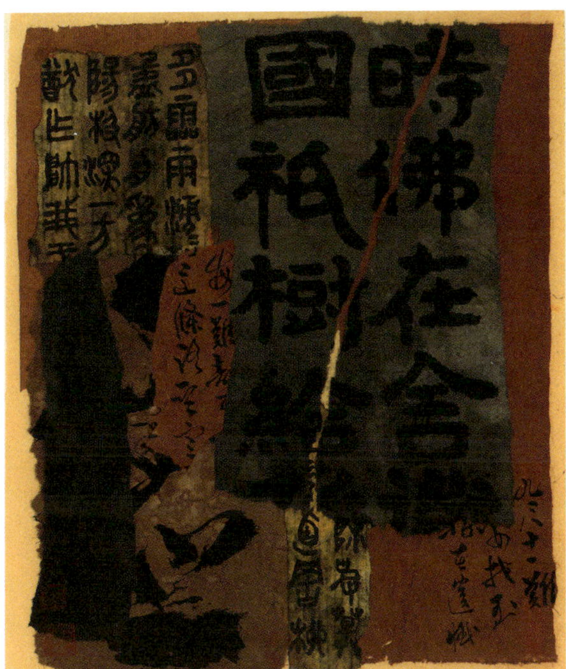

Cat.5 Qu Leilei, *Where Are You Going To?*, 1998. Ink and colour on paper

endowed them with new significance. The fragments of calligraphy in different styles are verses from an original poem composed by the artist in 1998:

Where Are You Going To?
When you are facing a historical choice,
There are ninety-nine roads you can take, but
Maybe only one of them really belongs to you.
And on the one you choose
There might be eighty-one disastrous events,
Any one of them could break you into pieces.
However, you must find that way
And go on with it firmly,
Otherwise you will regret it
And waste your life in the end.
In this world there are very few
Who can achieve what they want to,
That is the reason.[22]

Qu Leilei's calligraphic collages are made from torn pieces of paper with different tones of colour wash. To secure the various collage shapes in place, he uses traditional Chinese mulberry paper produced in Wenzhou, Zhejiang province, which is water soluble and more durable than rice paper. The figures and shapes were not cut out, but torn apart by hand. Qu Leilei prefers a torn edge, more in keeping with the work's spontaneous and expressive nature. The lack of precision with the shape and placement of the mulberry paper creates a more subtle effect. In particular some coloured pieces, written in archaic Chinese script, have been torn apart and rearranged to create a remarkable image recalling a fragmentary stele. Unlike other collage makers who often use acrylic for colouring and gluing materials, Qu Leilei uses Chinese ink and paints for colouring. Many of the colours resemble the pigments of ancient Chinese landscapes, from blue grey and beige to yellow ochre, brown and soft rust red. It is not gluing, but mounting that produces a beautiful, seamless, calligraphic collage. This method also forms rich textures over the surface of collage works. Perceived as general signs of Chinese history, the archaic scripts create the impression of meditating on the past.

Ink painting

After 1995 Qu Leilei shifted his principal focus from calligraphic collages to ink paintings. In his choice of medium, he proves to be well aware of tradition – ink on paper carries many concepts of philosophy and cosmology. His study in London has given him a very strong grounding in Western approaches to art, but an embrace of European painting does not result in a complete rejection of Chinese artistic conventions. Qu Leilei's ink paintings are a medium to frame ideas and narrate stories, especially in his serial works. Every aspect of his work reflects the aesthetic issues and cultural significance that he is currently exploring. His whole life is involved with considering aesthetic issues – after exploring one as far as he wishes, he moves on to another. His figural painting is inspired by the timeless beauty of human form celebrated in Western art, but offers a contemporary interpretation of the subject, drawing on two visual languages. One is abstract and freely expressive, the other concrete and meticulous. Both pay great attention to the rhythmic lines and shapes, revealing a true mastery of light and shadow.

Depicting physical beauty

Qu Leilei believes that women are God's most beautiful creation: nothing will stop him from portraying them brilliantly again and again. He explores the female figure in drawings and numerous studies, executed with ink and brush or pencil and watercolour (Fig.13, Cats 13–16). His nude paintings have a distinctive aesthetic appeal. The female body in his detailed academic nudes recalls Hellenistic sculpture and Renaissance art. Qu Leilei's

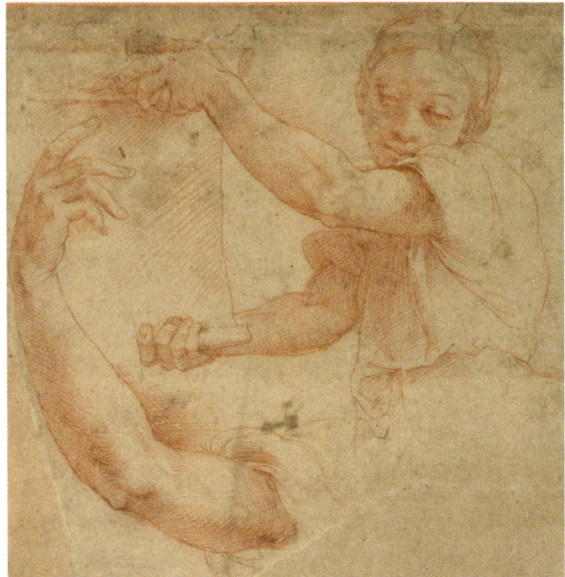

Fig.14 Raphael (1483–1520), *Studies of a figure holding a scroll and a raised right arm*, *c.*1511–14. Red chalk, 20.2 × 21.7 cm. Vienna, Albertina 17573

combination of accurate anatomy, classical posture and dignified nudity has established a distinguished, highly individual style.

If I have got the right feeling, I can paint again and again; the eternal beauty [of the female nude] lies in its rhythm, moving like waves.
Qu Leilei, description of a nude study, May 2011

Nude painting is essentially foreign to Chinese artists, but its history in the West extends back for centuries, through the Renaissance and into classical antiquity. Renaissance artists started to produce a wide range of images depicting the nude from 1490 onwards. Studying the human skeleton and drawing the structure of muscles from famous statues of flayed figures was standard practice in the art schools in Europe throughout the eighteenth and nineteenth centuries. Female models, naked or clothed, were barred from the French Academy until 1759, however, when clothed models were permitted, and across nineteenth-century Europe only male models were allowed at life-drawing classes.[23]

Unlike classical Western art, traditional Chinese painting offers no space for the genre until the twentieth century. Liu Haisu 劉海粟 (1896–94) faced a threat from the local warlord to close his school for using nude models in his Shanghai art classes.[24] Images of the female nude by European and Japanese painters were reproduced by Chinese artists in the 1920s and 1930s.[25] From the early twentieth century the genre was also introduced to China though its first generation of expatriate artists. For instance, Sanyu 常玉 (1901–66), who studied in France, was well known for his female nudes, painted with the Chinese brush technique. In his work the lower parts, pelvic area and thighs of female figures were often inflated to make an erotic statement.[26] In 1988 an exhibition of relatively modest nude oil paintings in Beijing was rejected by communist officials as a display of Western decadence and closed down. It was the first time since 1949 that nude painting had seemed to be gaining more widespread appeal, the genre having been forbidden during the Cultural Revolution.[27] Chinese art students have painted nude models in classroom situations since at least 1914, but depicting a naked body for artistic display was deemed as pornographic until amendments to the law in April 1985.[28]

Abstract ink

Qu Leilei's early nude drawings combine a free-flowing line of movement with concise composition, achieved through confident use of ink and brush. The energy and enthusiasm stem from the artist's training in abstract figural painting and life-drawing classes in London. The outer contours of female nudes are portrayed in dark, bold lines. The three-dimensional volume of the forms is modelled through shading, executed by ink wash (Cats 7–10). In *Standing Figure I* (Cat.10) the female body is composed in a gentle S-curve and the anatomy has been simplified.

In Qu Leilei's British landscape drawings (Cats 17–21), the calligraphic linear drawing and ink shading correspond to that of abstract figures (Cats 12–16). Qu Leilei has travelled widely around Britain, producing many drawings and sketches that portray a vivid feeling for nature. His abstract British landscape paintings are excellent examples, combining the rural tranquillity of the countryside with an unsettled, ever-changing climate. He spends many hours walking through the countryside, taking time to observe and experience seasonal changes in nature.

The artist's knowledge is shown through his skilful ways of painting light and shadow. He applies expressive, sweeping and calligraphic brushstrokes to give the landscape atmospheric effects and poetic interpretation. One beautifully calligraphic example is his spring landscape with serpentine grasslands and trees (Cat.18); here the overall use of muted

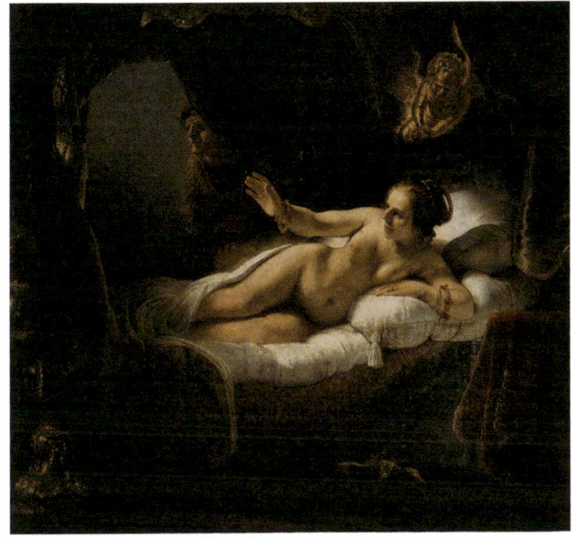

15

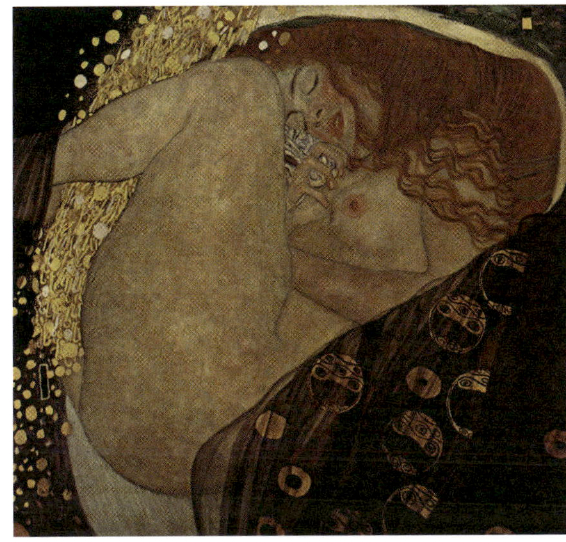

16

Fig.15 Rembrandt van Rijn (1606–1669), *Danaë*, 1636. Oil on canvas, 185 × 203 cm. Hermitage Museum, St Petersburg, Russia

Fig.16 Gustav Klimt (1862–1918), *Danaë*, 1907. Oil on canvas, 77 × 83 cm. Galerie Würthle, Vienna

Cat.22 Qu Leilei, *Danaë*, 2016 Ink on paper

tones created by light ink wash conveys a serene, pastoral setting. In a summer scene of the evocative Cornish coastline, gentle waves and sailing ships create a rhythmic and picturesque seascape (Cat.19). The delightful autumn landscape takes the Radcliffe Camera – one of the iconic buildings of the University of Oxford, especially painted for this exhibition – as its major theme (Cat.20).

Qu Leilei's work offers a deeply individual view of nature and history. For instance, the winter landscape of Stonehenge shows the prehistoric monument dwarfed by a vast sky with ominous grey clouds, lending an unsettled, transient feeling to the piece. The sense of immense time and space is echoed by the haunting inscription on the work: 'Where is the truth of the world? Looking back, thousands of years of history in Stonehenge' (Cat.21).

Refined figure painting

In contrast to his abstract drawings, Qu Leilei's highly refined nudes employ the *gongbi* style and introduce a greater sense of monumentality. The *gongbi* (meticulous brush) technique uses elaborate brushstrokes that delimit details very precisely, and dates back as far as the Tang Dynasty (618–906 AD). It is uniformly thick, even wiry, defining boundaries around figures and objects. *Gongbi* strove for extremely meticulous realism, achieved by painstakingly slow work of fine brushstrokes and shading in ink and colour. However, Qu Leilei's figural paintings differ from those traditional meticulous ink paintings in using the Western technique of chiaroscuro. At the same time Hellenistic and Roman art offered him rich inspiration for creating sculptural illusions in figures depicted with ink and brush. In such works Qu Leilei discovered a way to embrace tradition as well as innovation, and so created his signature style.

Since Qu Leilei settled in London in 1985 exposure to Western art, especially classical sculpture and Italian Renaissance painting, intensified his quest for perfection in the representation of the human body. The artist's nude painting is influenced by Michelangelo's style which often idealised the human

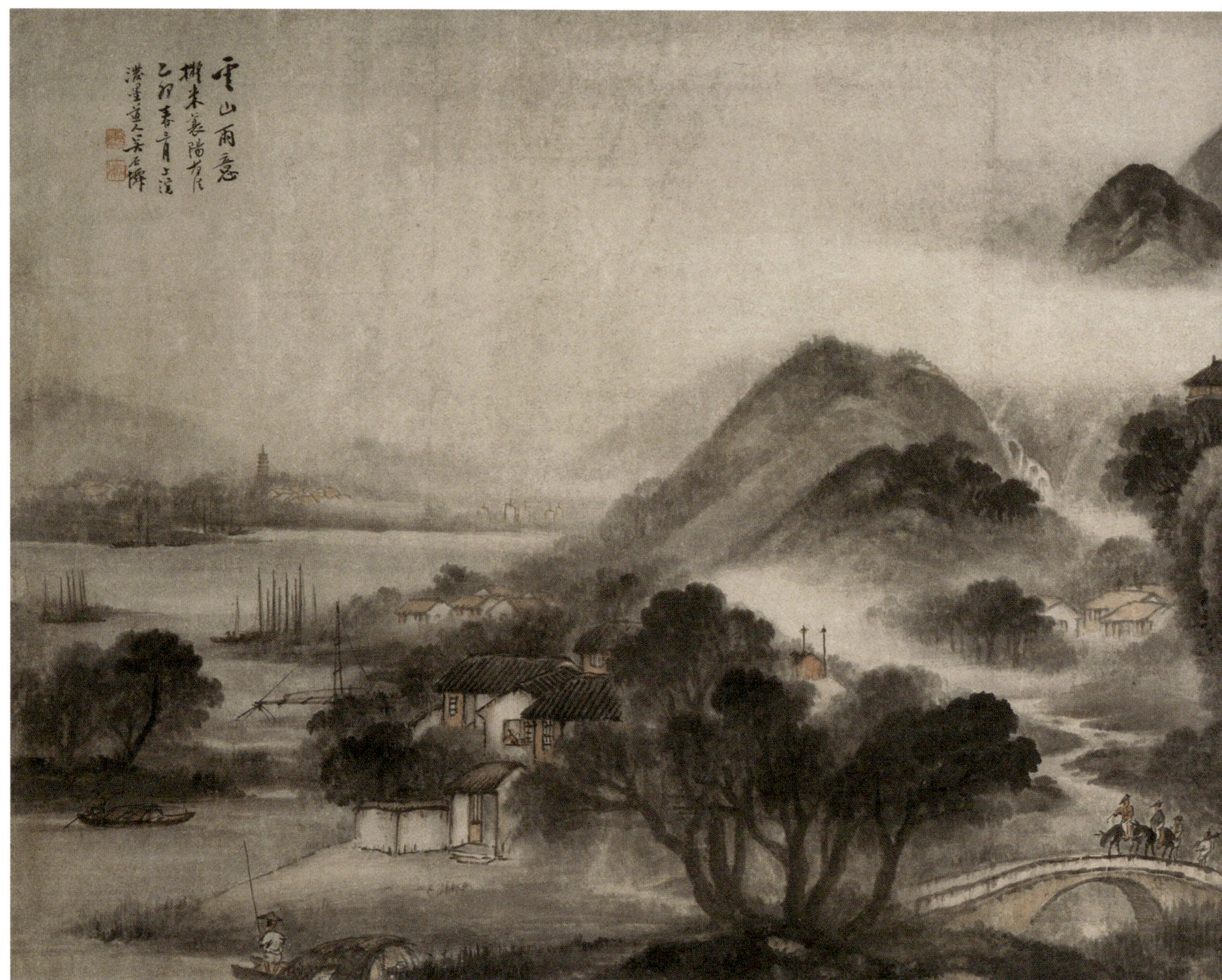

form, changing realistic or natural proportions to be more beautiful or perfect,[29] while the forms he deploys are informed by close observation of human anatomy, influenced by Raphael (Fig.14). Qu Leilei's work focuses on beauty, aesthetics, compositional harmony and balance. Likeness is less important than perfect realism in his nude paintings. Their anatomy is subtly articulated and their sculptural presence maintained. The compositional unity of a painting is integral to the power of its image, mastering careful observation and accurate depiction.

The *Reclining Nude (Danaë)* (Cat.22) is one of Qu Leilei's signature works in which he demonstrates his poetic virtuosity. The name 'Danaë' refers to a subject drawn from the genre of erotic mythologies in Western art.[30] Lying upon a magnificent expanse of oriental tapestry, the female nude in this painting is reminiscent of countless images portrayed by Giovanni Bellini, Titian and others. In its method of expressing light, this painting draws inspiration from Rembrandt's *Danaë* (Fig.15). Yet its style of composition is influenced by Klimt's work, which depicts a curled female figure encountering Zeus, transformed into a shower of gold (Fig.16). The nudity in Qu Leilei's ink paintings is tranquil and beautiful, an exquisite presentation of the ideal in all of its imagined loveliness; it is thus set apart from other Western interpretations, such as Klimt's extremely erotic portrayal. The transparency of the brushwork blends into the taste for flawless, porcelain skin and an oriental aesthetic.

In many of Qu Leilei's figural paintings the female nude rarely shows her face, but conceals her front and displays her back. It seems that Qu Leilei does not want to rely on facial expressions to show emotion, instead claiming the painter's power to bring the brushed figure to life through expression of light and shadow. He discovered the human figure early and understands all he needs to know of its construction. The *Seated Nude* (Cat.23) provides a crucial example of how he integrated the surfaces of the figure with their surroundings, important to works largely concerned with the relationship of figures to the background.

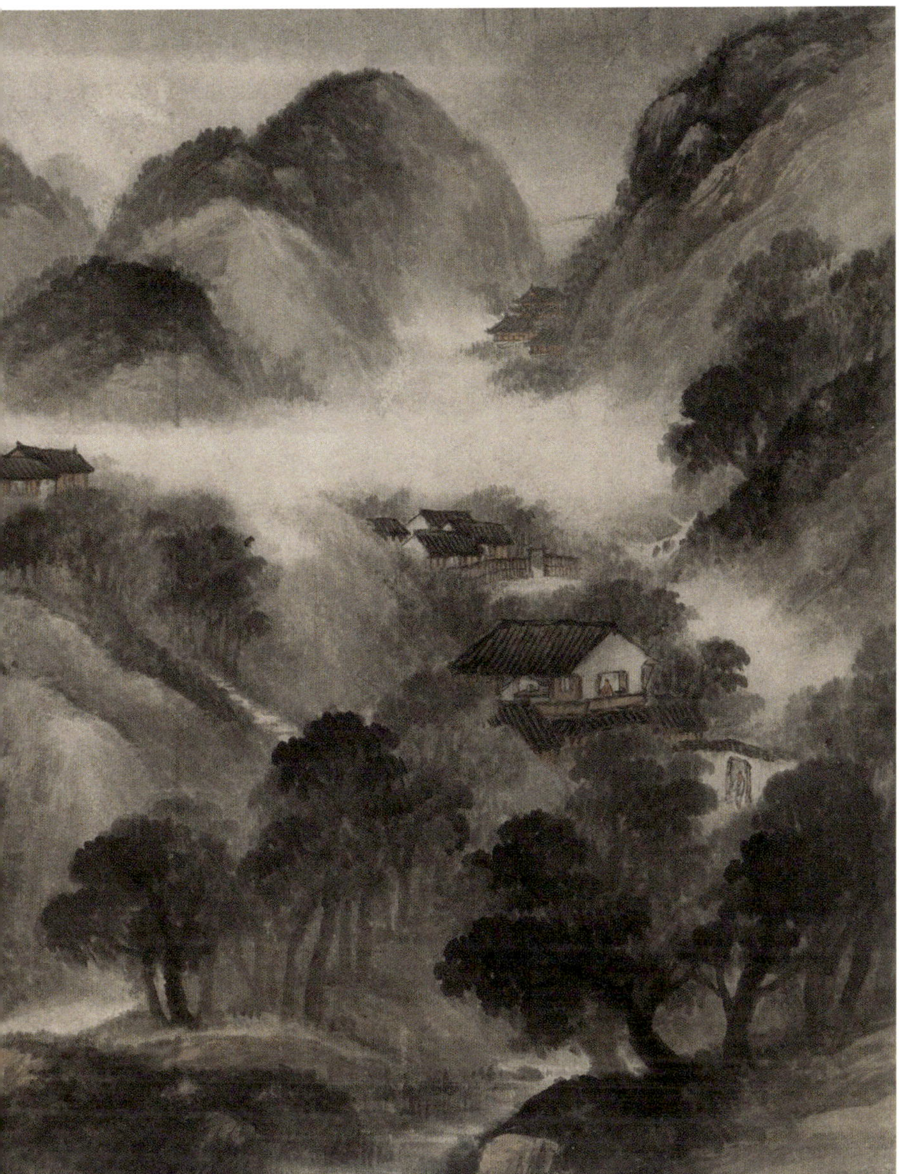

Fig.17 Wu Qingyun (d.1916), *Rain in the Cloudy Mountains*, 1915. Ink on paper, 45.7 × 96.5 cm. Ashmolean Museum, EA1963.3

The large figural painting is executed with meticulous brushwork, drawing from both the sculptures of classical antiquity and the realism of European oil painting. The grand hanging scroll, depicting a standing nude (Cat.24), was painted with high contrast in light and dark. Qu Leilei's love of beauty for its own sake, combined with his long and careful studies of human anatomy and Renaissance old masters, no doubt contribute to the extreme grace of his figures and the classical serenity of his theme and style. The viewer's eye is drawn to the female bodies, with all their youthful slenderness. The grey and ivory tones, grace of line and harmony of composition are attributes that immediately strike the beholder.

Light and shadow

Qu Leilei's figure painting is also about physicality. The light and shadow bear a metaphoric weight in their own right, and together they create a dramatic contrast within the space of the painting. The artist developed his individual style in monochrome ink by the creative use of chiaroscuro (pictorial representation in terms of light and shade without regard to colour). Interestingly, some evidence exists that chiaroscuro effects were used in ancient China, as seen from the Dunhuang mural paintings with the advent of Buddhism in the Six Dynasties period (220–589 AD). Traditionally Chinese painters did not make use of light in visual representation until the eighteenth century.[31] During the eighteenth and nineteenth centuries Chinese court painters interacted directly with European missionary-artists, from whom they learnt the laws of linear perspective and chiaroscuro of European painting. These were modified to suit the Chinese aesthetic and adopted to create the illusion of light and depth.[32]

The landscapes by Wu Qingyun from the Ashmolean's collection provide excellent examples of the use of chiaroscuro in the early twentieth-century Chinese ink painting. Wu Qingyun 吳慶雲 (d.1916), also known as Wu Shixian 吳石仙, painted landscapes in heavy ink after the styles of the eleventh-century painter Mi Fu and his fellow native of Nanjing, the seventeenth-century artist Gong Xian 龔賢 (1618–89). Wu's use of Western-style chiaroscuro is more evident in the landscape hanging scrolls (Fig.17).

In contrast to his predecessors, Qu Leilei applied the chiaroscuro to his ink painting in a very different way. 'To regard light as dark' (計白當黑) describes the expression of light in traditional Chinese painting through a blank space in the work. Qu Leilei executed it in the other way around, preferring 'To regard dark as light' (計黑當白). That is, the artist reversed the usual relation between substance and emptiness, creating large spaces of black (instead of white) emptiness. He strikes a fine balance between fullness and void, thick and thin, dense and sparse, moist and dry, curved and straight. As the art historian Michael Sullivan has observed, Qu Leilei's larger figure painting shows how the Chinese medium of brush and ink, traditionally viewed as a linear art, can

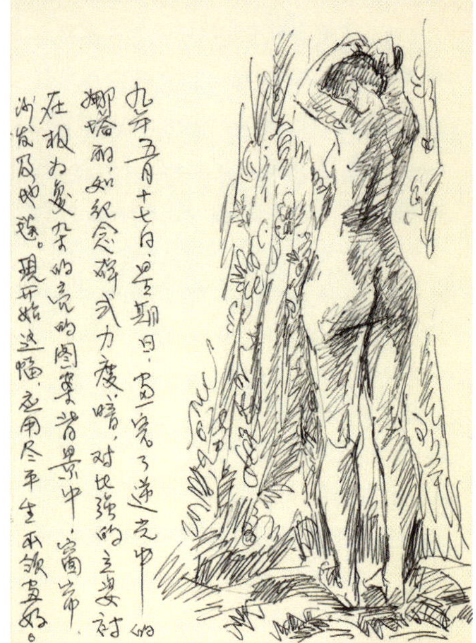

18

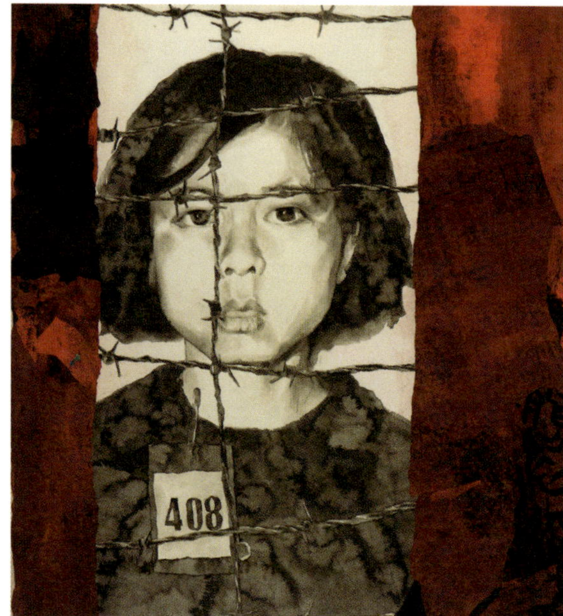

19

Fig.18 Qu Leilei, *Nude Study*, 2009. Ink on paper

Fig.19 Qu Leilei, *A Cambodian Girl*, 2005. Ink and colour on paper with collage. Ashmolean Museum, EA2005.82

through skilful and extremely subtle gradations of light and shade produce those tactile values that the American art historian Bernard Berenson thought to be at the heart of all good art: 'not only a satisfying contrast of texture, but an interplay of mass and line, stillness and movement...'[33]

Before painting with brush and ink, Qu Leilei starts to sketch a nude with charcoal. He adds outlines and details that he considers necessary and also defines the divisions of light and shadow. He often paints the nude close to life-size. The large scale offers greater scope for a variety of freely expressed techniques, as shown in the *Danaë*. Here he used short, textural strokes of hemp-fibre brushes – characteristic of Dong Yuan 董源 (fl.930s–60s) and reinterpreted by Wang Hui 王翬 (1632–1717) – to indicate the ornamental details of tapestry. Qu Leilei worked intensively on the detail, mainly using ink and brush. The brightest light shone on to the female body in the foreground, then, working from mid-tones to darks and to lights over background, the artist toned down some of the foreground colour to refine and unify colours in other areas. The shading of a nude figure is very difficult to get perfect the first time, as the colours will change when the ink dries. In one of his sketchbooks featuring nude studies (Fig.18), Qu Lelei wrote:

I need to paint very carefully to produce subtle shades through the light and dark contrast, focusing on the relationship between the nude body and its background, the large backlighting area and the bright monumental female body as well. The female body should be slightly darker but not tedious, while the background should be slightly brighter with variable tones. When rendering with shadows one after the other, it requires more confident and skilful brush handling, as rice paper is very fragile and prone to tearing after multiple ink washes. To produce a good painting, we need to balance the relationship between simplicity and complexity, light and shadow, void and substance, softness and hardness.[34]

The elaborately painted nudes exemplify Qu Leilei's ability to fuse contemporary models with classical aesthetics. In *Reclining Nude* (Cat.25), he painted a lounging female who rests on her left elbow and turns her face away; her anatomy is freely interpreted. The painting refers to Hellenistic and Roman marble sculptures, and to the realism achieved by Renaissance European masters in oil paintings; both genres converge in Qu Leilei's ink art. The heightened beauty of this female body is expressed through a sophisticated manipulation of light and shadow. The same subject appears in various paintings. These beautiful forms resemble marble, yet are fresh, living and breathing, radiant and glowing.

Friendship in art

In 2005 Qu Leilei held a solo exhibition in the Ashmolean Museum of Art and Archaeology featuring the series 'Everyone's Life is an Epic'. The display featured individual portraits to depict the everyday life of different people in the contemporary world, ranging from a Tibetan woman to an English farmer, a Chinese dancer to a British diplomat. The figures were characterised by light and shadow in brush and ink. Qu Leilei frequently uses vibrant colour collage as the background to his portraits, the strong contrast with the monochrome figure creating dramatic visual effects. *A Cambodian Girl* (Fig.19) is one example in which striking colour contrast produces a powerful, evocative image.

Qu Leilei developed a scientific approach to human anatomy and used chiaroscuro technique to represent light and shadow in his figure paintings. *The Future Remains in Our Own Hands* (Cat.26) is a work from his 'Here and Now Facing the Future' series. Its essential characteristic is an emphasis on

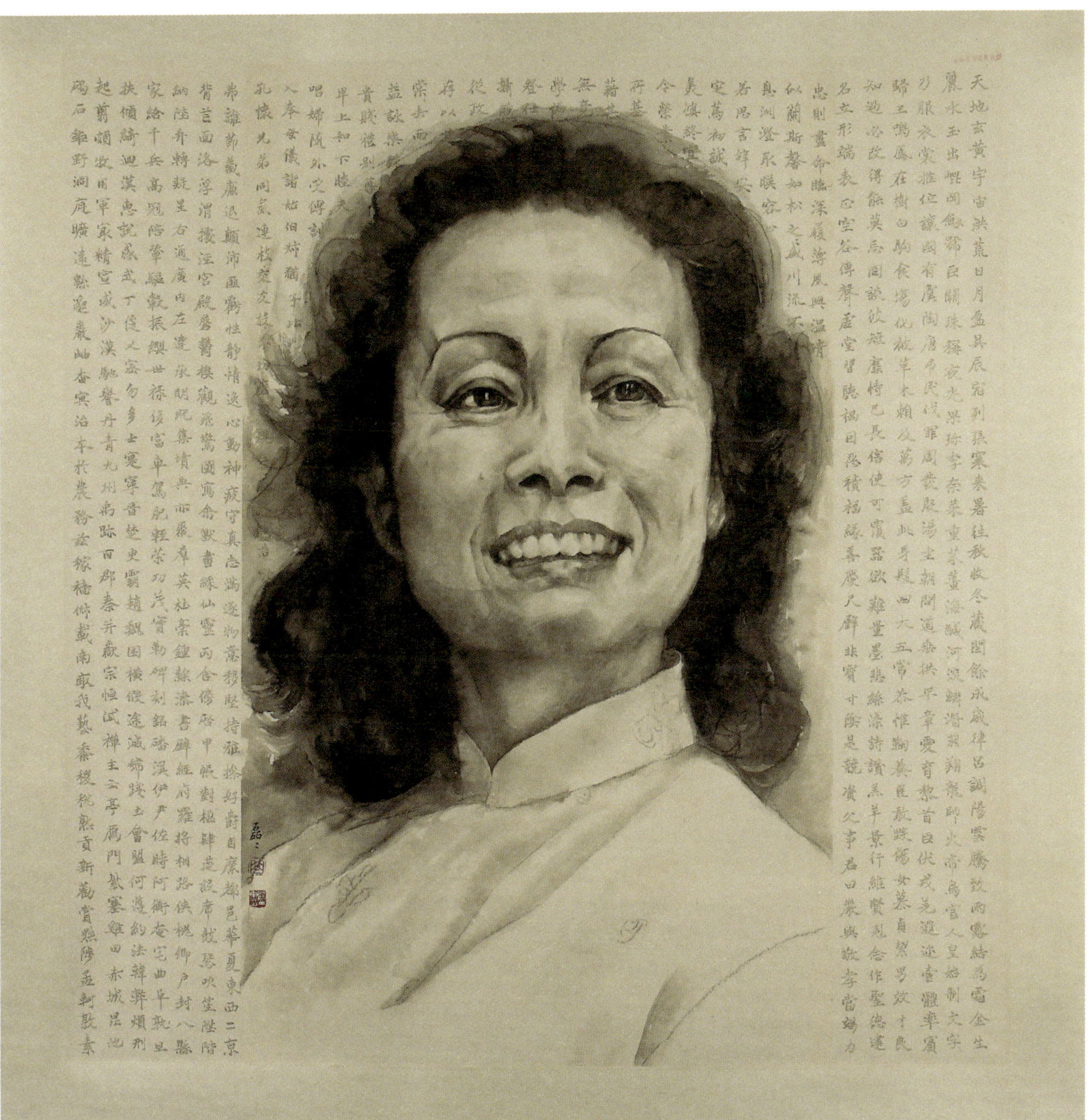

Fig.20 Qu Leilei, *Portrait of Khoan Sullivan* (1919–2003), 2002. Ink on paper. AshmoleanMuseum, EA2015.276

clear separation between light and dark, the simple structure conveying the artist's intense emotion. The images of a variety of hands reveal the accuracy of his anatomical knowledge. We can clearly see how the knuckles across the back of the baby's hands are buried in flesh, indicated by dimples.

Another work, *Friendship* (Cat.27), portrays the hands of Qu Leilei's wife Caroline and Professor Michael Sullivan. Born on 29 October 1916 in Toronto, Sullivan was a pioneering scholar and a leading international collector of modern and contemporary Chinese art. He read architecture at Corpus Christi College, Cambridge in 1936, then went to southwest China in 1939 to drive trucks for the Red Cross. There he met and married Khoan in 1943 and built lifelong friendships with many Chinese artists, including Pang Xunqin 龐薰琹 (1906–85), Ding Cong 丁聰 (1916–2009), Guan Shanyue 關山月 (1912–2000), Wu Zuoren 吳作人 (1908–97) and Chang Dai-chien 張大千 (1899–1983). Khoan gave up a promising career in medicine in China to support Sullivan's art history pursuits in Britain and America. She made an important contribution to the richness of their collection by establishing bridges between Sullivan and Chinese artists. Over the last seven decades the Sullivans built up a rich collection of modern and contemporary Chinese art, accommodating diverse styles and media. In 2013 the Ashmolean Museum received this collection comprising more than 450 Chinese paintings and the Sullivan archives, bequeathed by the late Professor Michael Sullivan. The bequest included portraits of Khoan and Michael and other paintings by Qu Leilei (Figs 20 and 21).

In both portraits Qu Leilei abandoned colours, preferring a monotone typical of literati taste. Literati art had achieved high status in Chinese painting for over 1,000 years, beginning in the Tang Dynasty (618–906 AD), when scholar elites and masters of literature and poetry often tried their hands at painting. Later, in the Song Dynasty, Su Shi 蘇軾 (1037–1101) and Mi Fu 米芾 (1051–1107), scholar officials, calligraphers and amateur painters, formulated a new artistic ideal. They believed that the style of the painting was more important than a

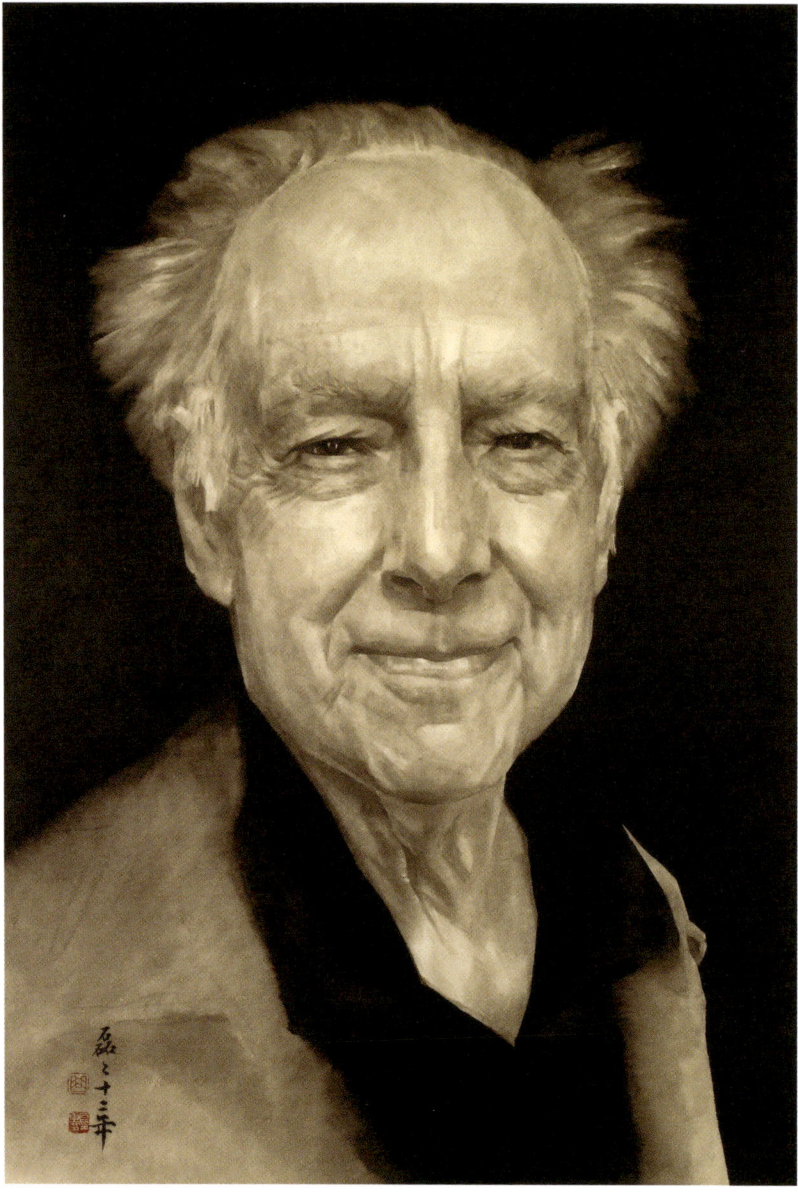

Fig.21 Qu Leilei, *Portrait of Michael Sullivan* (1916–2013), 2012. Ink on paper. Ashmolean Museum, EA2012.20

realistic interpretation of the subject.[35] However, it was not until the Yuan Dynasty (1206–1368), a period when China was under Mongol control, that literati painting became widespread.[36]

The portraits of the Sullivans, in which Qu Leilei successfully combined literati tradition with European art style, marked his development and maturation as a contemporary ink painter. In Khoan's portrait, the bright background with its beautiful calligraphy made her image stand out. Her black hair and the traditional *qipao* she wears – a stylish and feminine dress that originated in the Manchu banner gown – provided a clue to her Chinese background. Always with a smile upon her face, Khoan's lively and effervescent personality was well captured with brush and ink. In Michael's portrait Qu Leilei used dark background and concentrated on the details of facial features to show his generosity and kindness.

Their friendship began in Beijing in 1980, at the second exhibition of the 'Stars Group' in 1980. When Qu Leilei settled in England in 1985, they had many encounters. The idea of depicting Michael's and Caroline's hands as a symbol of friendship was conceived during a visit to the home of their friend Clico Kingsley, where they met Sullivan with his young friends. In his late period at Oxford Michael Sullivan was working on his new edition of *Arts of China*, assisted by young scholars and graduate students whom he called his 'little animal friends'. Hands are universal visual symbols; Sullivan later commented that 'surely the human hand is one of the most difficult things to draw, but not only does he [Qu Leilei] draw hands beautifully; he makes of them a powerful image expressive of thoughts, feelings, humanity and love'.[37] Qu Leilei's hand paintings are strong and powerful, in many ways resembling sculptures. This effect gave his drawings more solidity and depth, characterising his later development in figure painting.

Preserving cultural memory

From 2011 onwards Qu Leilei started his series of works called 'A Thousand Years of Empire'. In this

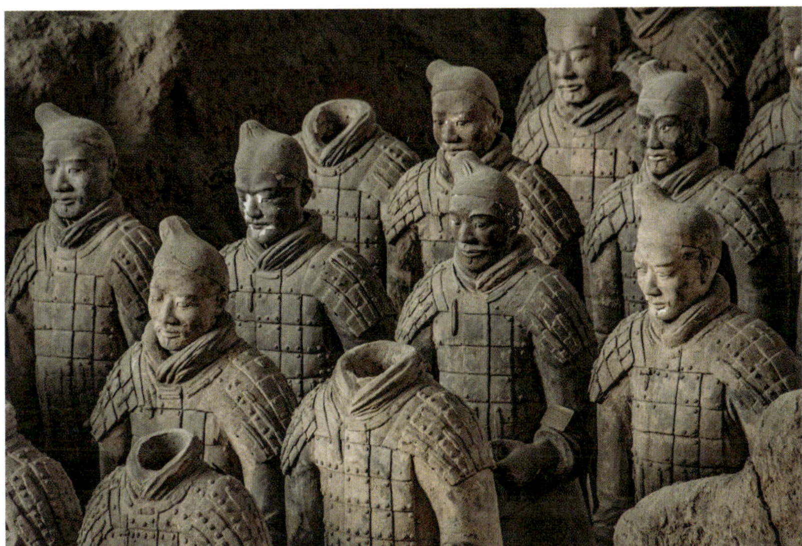

Fig.22 Terracotta warriors, Lingtong, Shaanxi. Emperor Qinshihuang's Mausoleum site Museum, Xi'an, Shaanxi Province

he has drawn inspiration from the historical legacy of early imperial China to explore the cultural roots of Chinese painting. Alongside rediscovery of tradition, the 'Empire' series reflects a shift away from the physical preoccupations of aesthetic thought towards a more historical, culturally-based interpretation of humanity.

Qu Leilei formulated the political significance of the soldier figure by relating it to the iconic image of terracotta warriors – the funerary statues discovered in the necropolis of Emperor Qin Shihuang (259–210 BC) in Xi'an, Shaanxi province. This remarkable discovery first came to light in March 1974, when farmers uncovered strange figures while digging a well near the old Chinese capital of Xianyang. In burial pits close to the main tomb, archaeologists have discovered thousands of pottery figures of courtiers, warriors, officials, musicians and acrobats. These life-size terracotta soldiers were made with a very sophisticated technique, creating a model army to protect the emperor in the afterlife.[38] The first emperor, known as a cruel and ruthless tyrant, built a highly organised, mobile and powerful army in unifying China. In addition to constructing the first lengths of the Great Wall, the tyrannical ruler standardised the nation's script, currency and system of measurements.

Ancient objects, especially artefacts obtained through archaeological excavation, have become a primary source for the creation of art by contemporary Chinese artists. The authenticity of ancient artefacts makes their social and cultural value emotionally persuasive, and the majority of their images used in art show a strong bias towards traditional Chinese culture and nationalist pride. Yet some of the contemporary paintings drawn from this historical legacy, including individual portraits of Qin terracotta soldiers by Ye Xue (b.1962), the study of silk garments from the Mawangdui Han tomb by Guo Liming (b.1963) and the embroidered image based upon the Mawangdui funerary silk banner by Liu Dahong (b.1962), are charged with political cynicism. Qu Leilei's historical legacy paintings are filled with powerful social criticism; each brushstroke expresses intense emotion. *The Soldier* (Cat.28) and *The Invincible* (Cat.29) depict the cultural trauma of institutionalised personality, through reference to the standardised terracotta soldiers, destined to serve as an underground army in the afterlife of the first emperor.

'Brush and ink should keep with the times.' Qu Leilei often quotes Shitao's text and uses it as his guideline for art creation. His ink paintings are inspired by a philosophical and aesthetic tradition from Chinese history, but are equally influenced by the realism of Western art and Hellenistic sculpture. The fusion of such diverse genres essentially weaves the visual language of traditional ink painting. His art unarguably possesses evocative poetic qualities, especially in its creative use of poetry, calligraphy and painting.

Contemporary Chinese ink painting is becoming increasingly multicultural and trans-boundaries. Qu Leilei's achievement, and the context in which it took place, is succinctly conveyed by Michael Sullivan, art historian and friend. 'It was an explosion of Chinese art, in response to the challenge of the West, in which the Chinese could take what they wanted and needed from the West to express themselves. On one hand, there's fascination with Western art, on the other hand, the growing self-confidence of Chinese art.'[39] Qu Leilei's art shows how immigrant Chinese artists maintain a balance between Western influence and Chinese tradition, as well as accommodating multiple identities. On the one hand, his work reveals a lasting preoccupation with the historical legacy, in its diverse aspects; on the other, it illustrates the trend toward a fusion of artistic traditions.

End notes

1 Michael Sullivan, *Art and Artists of Twentieth-century China.* Berkeley, CA: University of California Press, 1996.

2 Shen Kuiyi, 'Concept to Context: The Theoretical Transformation of Ink Painting into China's National Art in the 1920s and 1930s', in Josh Yiu, ed., *Writing Modern Chinese Art, Historiographic Explorations.* Seattle: Seattle Art Museum, 2009, pp.44–51.

3 Chu-Tsing Li and J. H. Murphy, 'Liu Guosong and Modern Chinese Ink Painting', in Hong Kong Museum of Art, *Liu Guosong: A Universe of His Own.* Hong Kong: Leisure and Cultural Services Department, the Government of Hong Kong, 2004, 24–33.

4 Sullivan 1996, 52–7.

5 Sullivan 1996, 203.

6 Julia F. Andrews and Shen Kuiyi, *The Art of Modern China.* Berkeley, CA: University of California Press, 2012.

7 'Contemporary' here refers to the past four decades of new artistic production, the years since the end of the Cultural Revolution in 1976. Gao Minglu, *Total Modernity and the Avant-Garde in Twentieth-Century Chinese Art.* Boston: The MIT Press, 2011.

8 Gao Minglu, ed., *Inside Out: New Chinese Art.* New York: San Francisco Museum of Modern Art and Asia Society Galleries, 1998.

9 Jerome Silbergeld, *Outside In: Chinese x American x Contemporary Art.* New Haven: Yale University Press, 2009.

10 Maxwell K. Hearn, *Ink Art: Past as Present in Contemporary China.* New York: Metropolitan Museum of Art, 2013.

11 Melissa Chiu, *Breakout, Chinese Art outside China.* Milan: Charta, 2006.

12 Paul Gladson, 'Locating Displacement: Envisioning the Complex "Diasporization" of Contemporary Chinese Art', in Birgit Hopfener and Franziska Koch, eds, *Negotiating Difference, Contemporary Chinese Art in the Global Context.* Weimar: Verlag und Datenbank für Geisteswissenschaften, 2012, pp.243–57.

13 Interview with Qu Leilei, 7 November 2016.

14 Barefoot doctors were farmers who had received very basic medical and paramedical training. They worked in rural villages to promote basic hygiene, preventive healthcare and family planning, and to treat common illnesses during the Cultural Revolution.

15 Li Xianting, 'About the Stars Art Exhibition'. In Peggy Wang, ed., *Contemporary Chinese Art Primary Document* (MoMA primary documents). New York: The Museum of Modern Art, 2010, pp.11–13.

16 For immigrant Chinese artists see Wu Hung, *Contemporary Chinese Art.* London: Thames & Hudson, 2012, pp.276–308.

17 P. Fuller, 'Cecil Collins: A New Dawn? *Modern Painters 2* (1989), p.30.

18 Christine Poggi, *In defiance of painting: Cubism, futurism, and the invention of collage.* New Haven: Yale University Press, 1993.

19 The Fifth Moon Group was founded in Taiwan in 1956. Its important members include Liu Guosong, Feng Zhongrui, Zhuang Zhe, Chen Tingshi (1913–2002), Hu Qizhong (1927–2012) and other Taiwanese painters. They met regularly to appreciate and critique one another's work, The Fifth Moon artists also exhibited their works at art shows held in May of each year. Ink, acrylic and collage were used to produce vibrant images, steering traditional Chinese ink painting towards abstract expressionism. Although their movement began in Taiwan, their outlook from the very beginning was international.

20 The members included Chen Tingshi (1913–2002), Feng Zhongrui (b.1934), Hu Qizhong (1927–2012), Liu Guosong (b.1932), and Zhuang Zhe (b.1934). See Michael Sullivan, *The Meeting of Eastern and Western Art.* Berkeley and Los Angeles: University of California Press, 1997. Hong Kong Museum of Art, ed., *Liu Guo Song: A Universe of His Own.* Hong Kong: Hong Kong Museum of Art, 2004. Galerie du monde. [AQ no authors for this work (none in biblio ref either)? Author has just added 'ed' but by whom?] *Fong Chung Ray, A Retrospective.* Hong Kong: China Art Press, 2015.

21 William Willetts, *Chinese Calligraphy, Its History and Aesthetic Motivation.* Oxford: Oxford University Press, 1981. Calligraphy first came to be recognised as an art in China during the first century AD and established itself as such between the third and the sixth centuries. The earliest known form from Chinese writing, called oracle-bone script (*jiaguwen*), dates from the thirteenth to the eleventh centuries BC. Regular script (*kaishu*) is upright, with a simple clarity and elegance; it was first used in the post-Han period and perfected during the seventh and tenth centuries. Clerical Script (*li shu*) has a balance and gravitas. It evolved towards the end of the first millennium BC and remained in common use throughout the Han Dynasty (206 BC—220 AD). Running Script (*xingshu*), which also appeared in the post-Han period, was executed with sufficient speed to create a flow of line and a variety of form.

22 Michael Sullivan, *Modern Chinese Art, The Khoan and Michael Sullivan Collection.* Oxford: Ashmolean Museum, 2009.

23 Adriano Aymonino, 'Nature Perfected: The Theory & Practice of Drawing after the Antique', in Adriano Aymonino and Anne Varick Lauder, eds, *Drawn From the Antique, Artist & the Classical Ideal.* Sir John Soane's Museum, 2015, p.15.

24 Andrews and Shen 2012, p.67.

25 David Clarke, *Chinese art and its encounter with the world.* Hong Kong: Hong Kong University Press, 2012, p.124.

26 Leslie Jones, 'Sanyu, Chinese painter of Montparnasse'. *Anthropology and aesthetics* 35 (1999), pp.224–39.

27 Michael Sullivan, *Art and Artists of Twentieth Century China.* Berkeley, CA: University of California Press, 1996, p.45.

28 John A. Clark, *Modernities of Chinese Art.* Leiden, Boston: Brill, 2010, pp.61–75.

29 Frederick Hartt, *History of Italian Renaissance Art*, 3rd ed. New York: Harry N. Abrams, Inc., 1987, p.592.

30 In Greek mythology Danaë was the daughter of Acrisius. According to the prophecy, the son Danaë was destined to bear would be instrumental in the death of his grandfather Acrisius. The god Zeus, who always had an eye for female charms, was struck by Danaë's beauty and desired her. Karl Kilinski, *Greek Myth and Western Art, the Presence of the Past.* New York: Cambridge University Press, 2013.

31 Mary H. Fong, 'The Technique of "Chiaroscuro" in Chinese Painting from Han through Tang'. *Artisbus Asiae* 38 (1976), pp.91–127.

32 Petra ten-Doesschate Chu and Ning Ding, *Qing Encounters: Artistic Exchanges between China and the West.* Los Angeles: Getty Research Institute, 2015, pp.190–215.

33 Michael Sullivan, Preface. In *Qu Leilei. Brush Ink Light Shadow.* Beijing: National Art Museum of China, 2011, pp.13–14.

34 Qu Leilei, sketchbook, 2011.

35 Michael Sullivan, *The Arts of China*, 6th ed.). Berkeley, CA: University of California Press, 2008, p.148.

36 James Cahill, *Hills Beyond a River: Chinese Painting of the Yuan Dynasty, 1279–1368.* New York and Tokyo: Weatherhill, 1976, pp.4–6.

37 Sullivan 2011.

38 Jane Portal, *The First Emperor: China's Terracotta Army.* Cambridge, MA: Harvard University Press, 2007.

39 Michael Sullivan, speech at the Silicon Valley Asian Art Center, March 2012.

Bibliography

Adriano Aymonino. 'Nature Perfected: The Theory & Practice of Drawing after the Antique', in Adriano Aymonino and Anne Varick Lauder, eds, *Drawn From the Antique, Artist & the Classical Ideal.* Sir John Soane's Museum, 2015, p.15.

Julia F. Andrews and Shen Kuiyi, *The Art of Modern China.* Berkeley, CA: University of California Press, 2012.

Richard M. Barnhart, ed., *Three Thousand Years of Chinese Painting.* New Haven: Yale University Press, 1997.

James Cahill, *Hills Beyond a River: Chinese Painting of the Yuan Dynasty, 1279–1368.* New York and Tokyo: Weatherhill, 1976.

Melissa Chiu, *Breakout, Chinese Art outside China.* Milan: Charta, 2006.

John A. Clark, *Modernities of Chinese Art.* Leiden, Boston: Brill, 2010.

David Clarke, *Chinese art and its encounter with the world.* Hong Kong: Hong Kong University Press, 2012.

Fuller, P, 'Cecil Collins: A New Dawn?' *Modern Painters 2* (1989), p.30.

Galerie du monde, *Fong Chung Ray, A Retrospective.* China Art Press, 2015.

Gao Minglu, ed., *Inside Out: New Chinese Art.* New York: San Francisco Museum of Modern Art and Asia Society Galleries, 1998.

Gao Minglu, *Total Modernity and the Avant-Garde in Twentieth-Century Chinese Art.* Boston: The MIT Press, 2011.

Paul Gladston, 'Locating Displacement: Envisioning the Complex "Diasporization" of Contemporary Chinese Art', in Birgit Hopfener and Franziska Koch, eds, *Negotiating Difference, Contemporary Chinese Art in the Global Context.* VDG Weimar, 2012, pp.243–57.

Frederick Hartt, *History of Italian Renaissance Art*, 3rd ed. New York: Harry N. Abrams, Inc. 1987, p.592.

Maxwell K. Hearn, *Ink Art: Past as Present in Contemporary China.* New York: Metropolitan Museum of Art, 2013.

Hong Kong Museum of Art, *Liu Guo Song: A Universe of His Own.* Hong Kong: Hong Kong Museum of Art, 2004.

Birgit Hopfener and Franziska Koch, eds, *Negotiating Difference, Contemporary Chinese Art in the Global Context.* VDG Weimar, 2012.

Karl Kilinski, *Greek Myth and Western Art, the Presence of the Past.* New York: Cambridge University Press, 2013.

Leo Ou-Fan Lee, 'Across Trans-Chinese Landscapes: Reflections on Contemporary Chinese Cultures', in Gao Minglu, ed., *Inside Out: New Chinese Art.* New York: San Francisco Museum of Modern Art and Asia Society Galleries, 1998, pp.4–9.

Li Xianting, 'About the Stars Art Exhibition', in Peggy Wang, ed., *Contemporary Chinese Art Primary Document (MoMA Primary Documents).* New York: The Museum of Modern Art, 2010, pp.11–13.

Chu-Tsing Li and J. H. Murphy, 'Liu Guosong and Modern Chinese Ink Painting', in Hong Kong Museum of Art, *Liu Guosong: A Universe of His Own.* Hong Kong: Leisure and Cultural Services Department, the Government of Hong Kong, 2004, pp.24–33.

Robert D. Mowry, ed., *Modern and Contemporary Chinese Ink Paintings from the Chu-tsing Li Collection 1950–2000.* New Haven: Yale University Press, 2007.

Petra ten-Doesschate Chu and Ning Ding, *Qing Encounters: Artistic Exchanges between China and the West.* Los Angeles, Getty Research Institute, 2015.

Christine Poggi, *In defiance of painting: Cubism, futurism, and the invention of collage.* New Haven: Yale University Press, 1993.

Jane Portal, *The First Emperor: China's Terracotta Army.* Cambridge: Harvard University Press, 2007.

Jerome Silbergeld, *Outside In: Chinese x American x Contemporary Art.* New Haven: Yale University Press, 2009.

Michael Sullivan, *Art and Artists of Twentieth-century China.* Berkeley, CA: University of California Press, 1996.

Michael Sullivan, *The Meeting of Eastern and Western Art.* Berkeley, CA: University of California Press, 1997.

Michael Sullivan, *The Arts of China*, 6th ed. Berkeley, CA: University of California Press, 2008, p.148.

Michael Sullivan, *Modern Chinese Art, The Khoan and Michael Sullivan Collection.* Oxford: Ashmolean Museum Press, 2009.

Michael Sullivan, 'Preface', in *Qu Leilei. Brush Ink Light Shadow.* Beijing: National Art Museum of China, 2011, pp.13–14.

William Willetts, *Chinese Calligraphy, Its History and Aesthetic Motivation.* Oxford: Oxford University Press, 1981.

Wu Hung, *Contemporary Chinese Art.* London: Thames & Hudson, 2012, pp.276 –308.

Josh Yiu, *Writing Modern Chinese Art, Historiographic Explorations.* Seattle: Seattle Art Museum, 2009.

Qu Leilei
A Chinese Artist in Britain
Catalogue

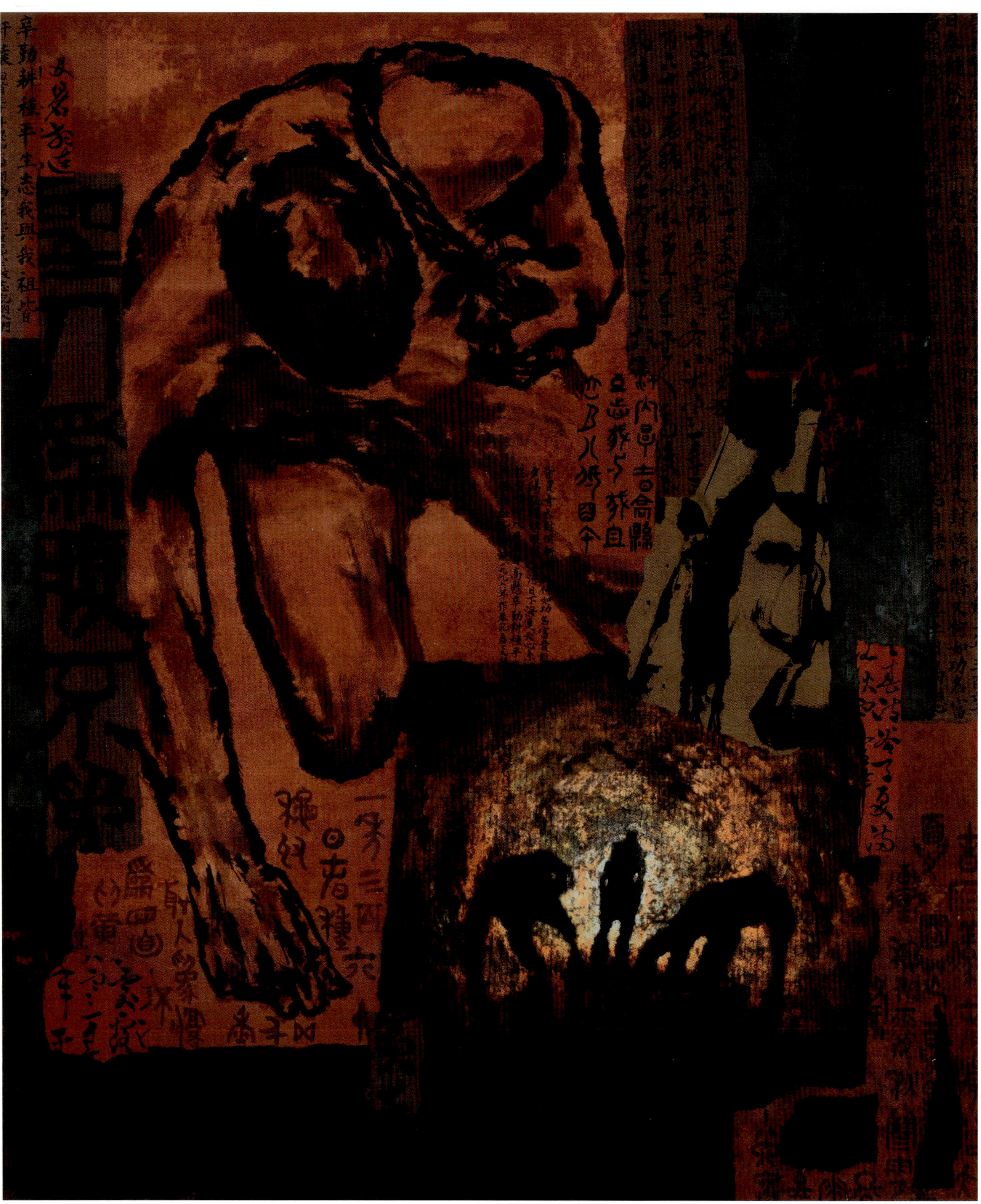
辛勤耕種平生志我與我祖皆

1
The Creator of Civilization
Ink and colour on paper
117 × 99 cm
1994
Collection of the artist

Inscription:
春雨驚春請穀天
夏滿芒夏暑相連
秋處露秋寒霜降
冬雪雪冬小大寒
一年三百六十日
春種秋收五千年
聖人為腹不為目
面向黃土背青天
封侯斬將又何如
功名富貴能幾番
夕陽馳暉轉眼過
江河日下海連天
心系天地能自悟
汗入厚土日高懸
辛勤耕種平生志
我與我祖皆軒轅

Seal 1 磊磊 *Leilei*
Seal 2 天問 *Tianwen*
Seal 3 東西南北 *Dong xi nan bei*
Seal 4 平生一片心 *Pingsheng yi pian xin*
Seal 5 野風 *Yefeng*
Seal 6 曲磊磊畫印 *Qu Leilei huayin*
Seal 7 閑雲 *Xianyun*
Seal 8 今日荷開 *Jinri hekai*
Seal 9 雁北飛 *Yan beifei*
Seal 10 有雨兼風 *Youyu jianfeng*
Seal 11 水天 *Shuitian*
Seal 12 鳥空啼 *Niao kongti*
Seal 13 暢神 *Changshen*
Seal 14 囊中無錢 *Langzhong wuqian*

2
Song of Four Seasons
Collage, ink and colour on mulberry bark paper
39 × 25 cm
1994
Collection of the artist

Seal 1: 曲 *Qu*
Seal 2: 磊磊画印 *Leilei huayin*
Seal 3: 野风 *Yefeng*
Seal 4: 雁北飞 *Yan bei fei*

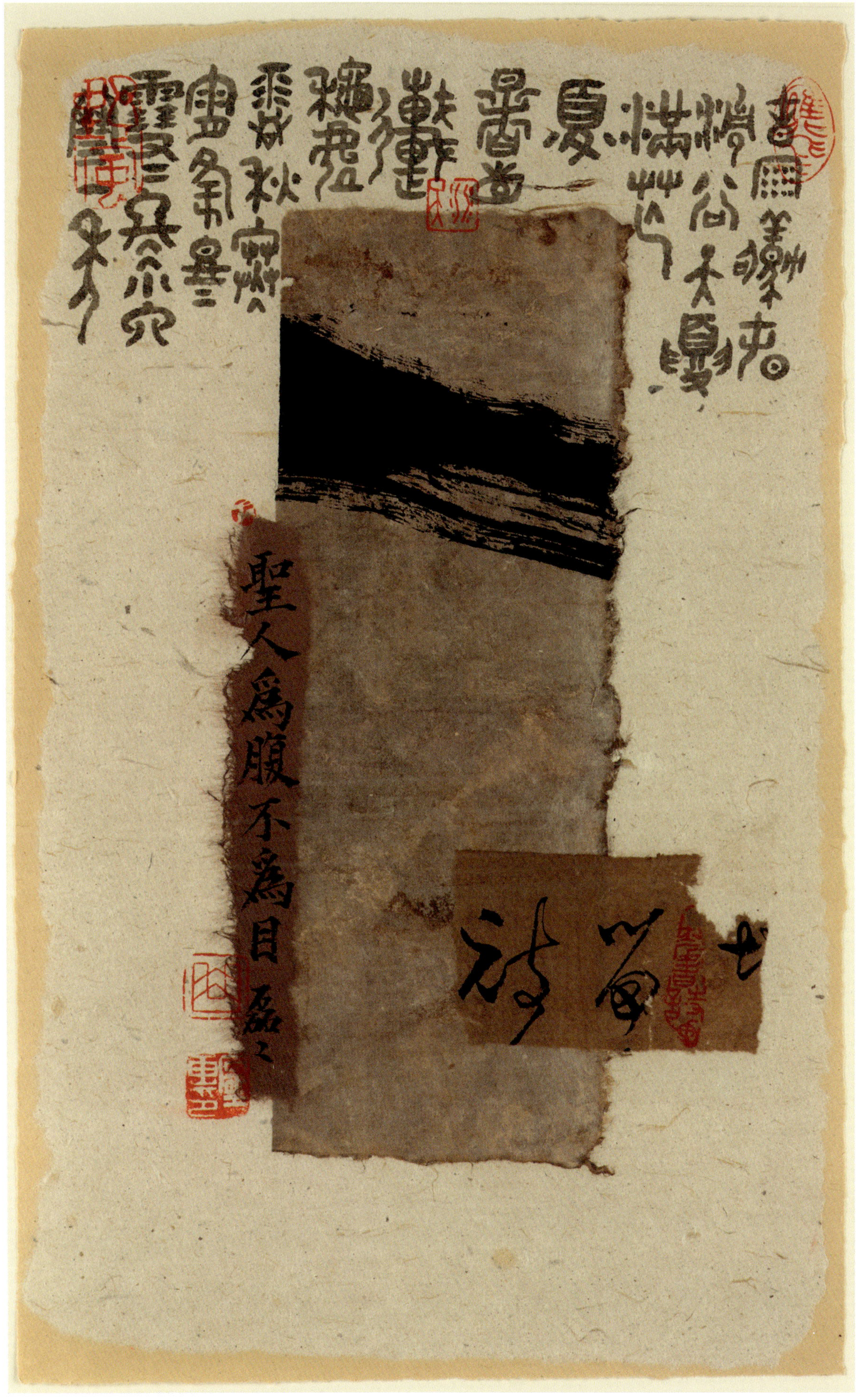

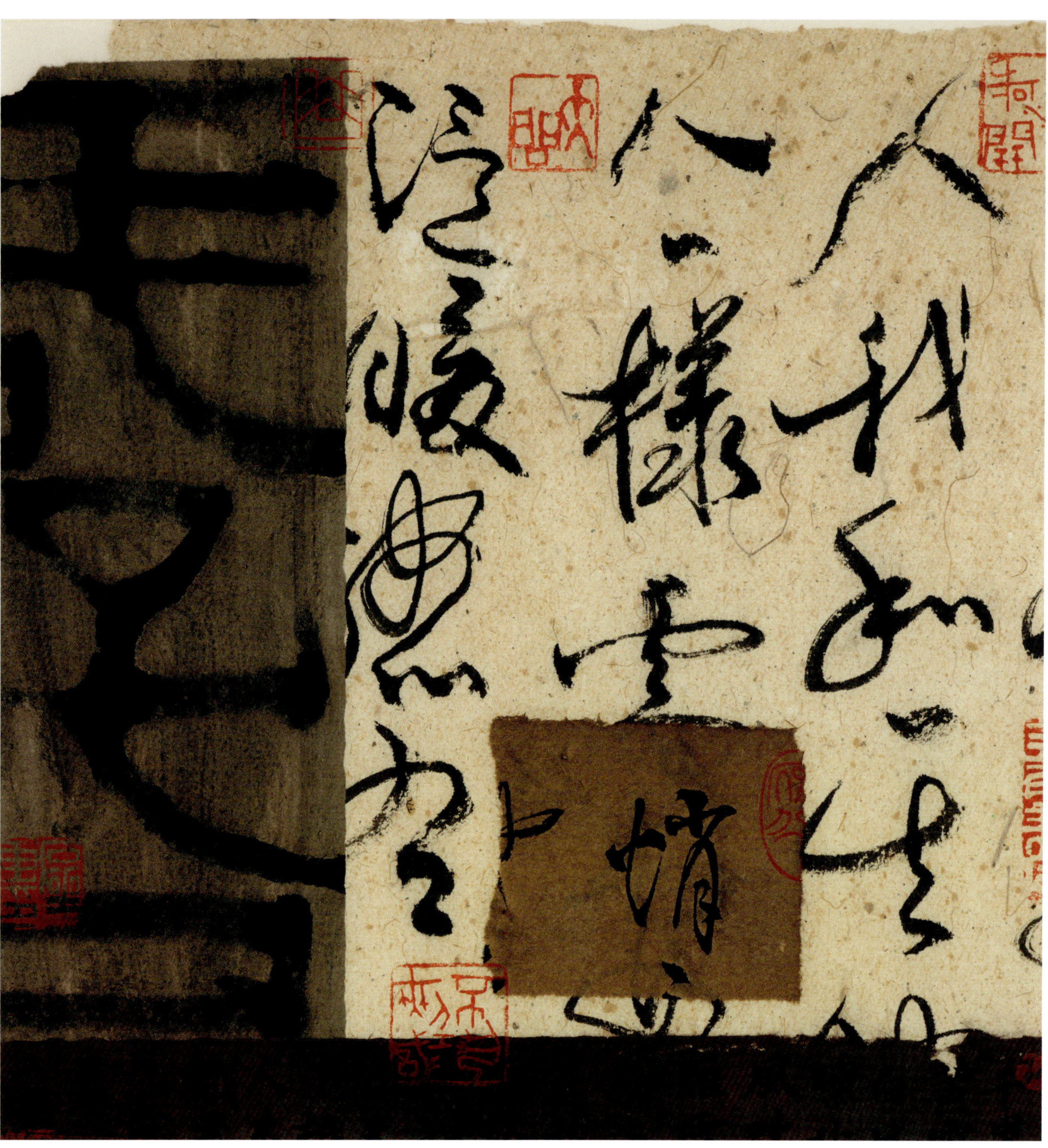

3
The Gentleman
Ink and colour on paper
34 × 23 cm
1994
Collection of the artist
Seal 1: 天問 *Tianwen*
Seal 2: 荷開 *Hekai*
Seal 3: 磊磊畫印 *Leilei huayin*
Seal 4: 曲 *Qu*

4
Blade of Light
Ink and colour on paper
69 × 49 cm
1998
Collection of the artist

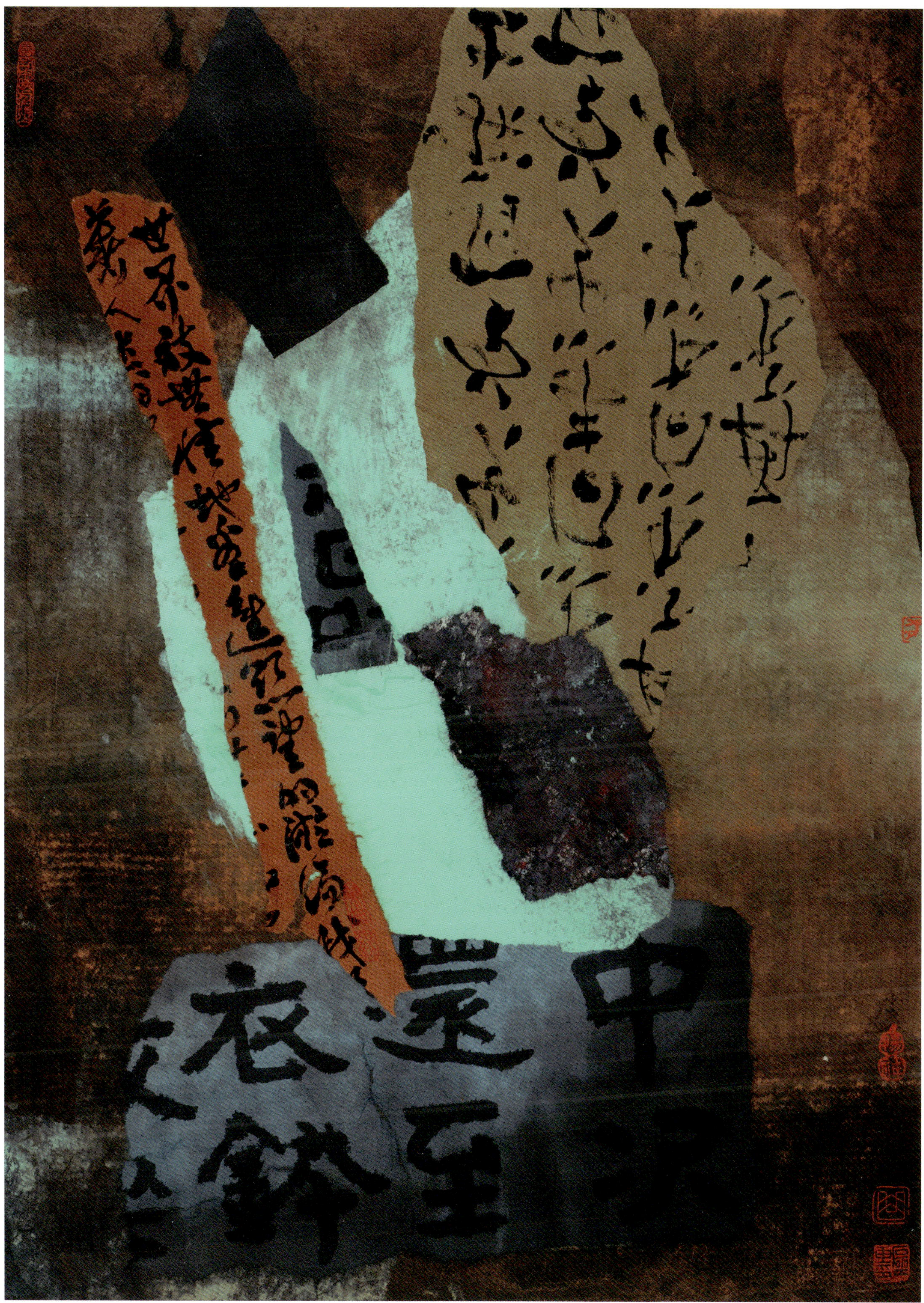

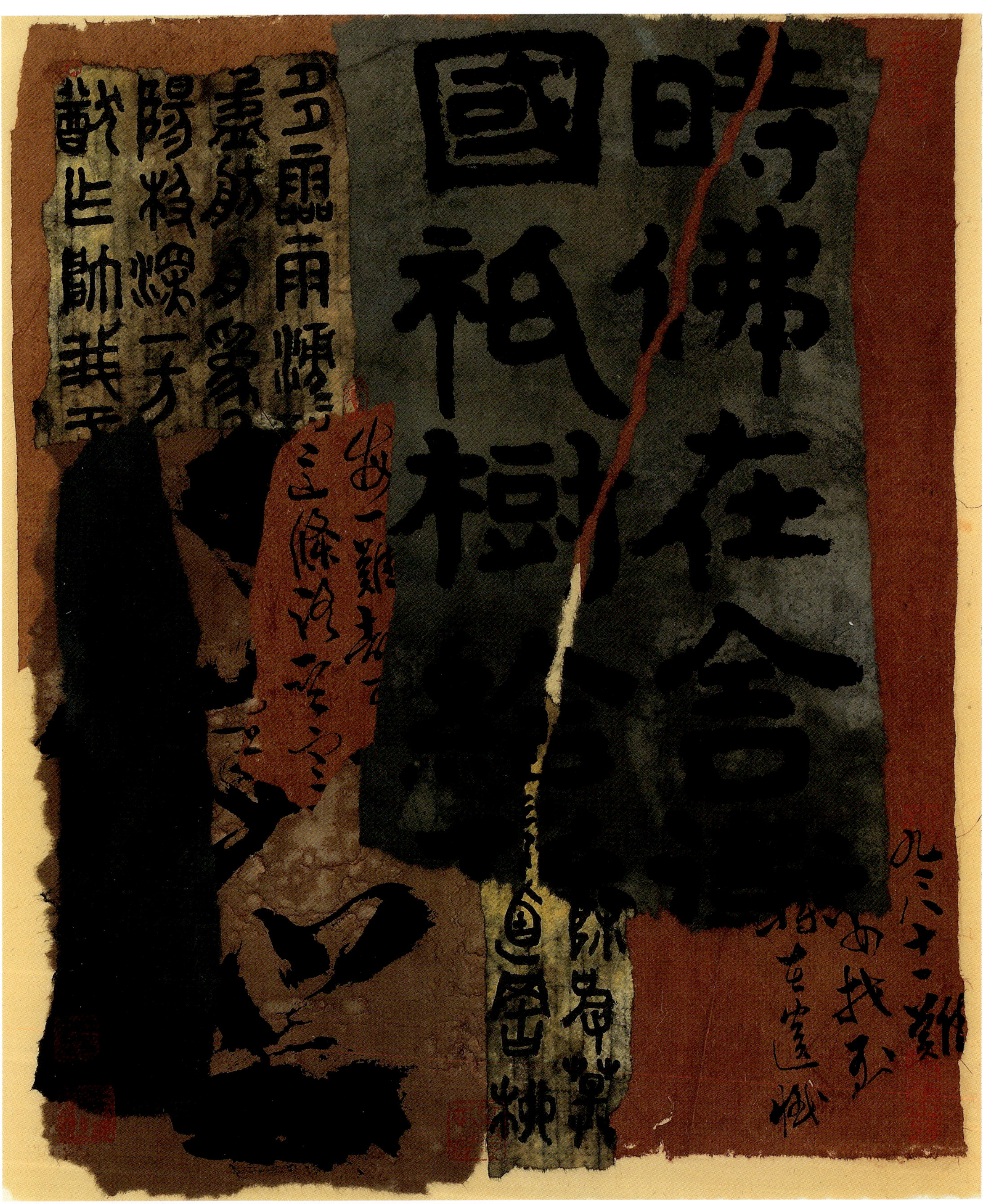
時佛在
國祇樹

5
Where Are You Going To?
Ink and colour on paper
51 × 42.6 cm
1998
EA2015.271
Sullivan Bequest

6
I Know
Ink and colour on paper
45.5 × 43 cm
2001
EA2015.272
Sullivan Bequest

Seal: 野风 Yefeng

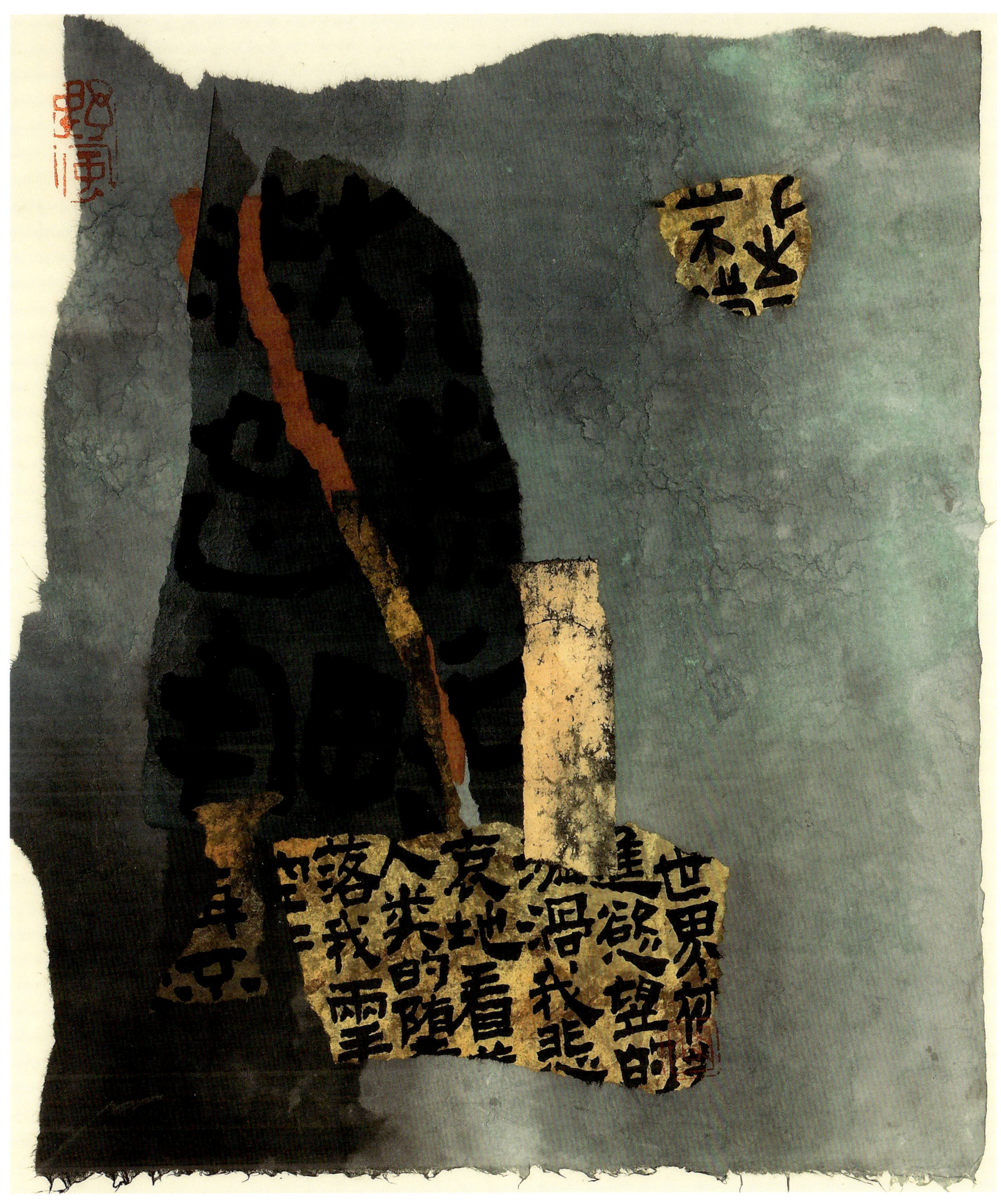

7
Kneeling Girl
Ink on paper
45.5 × 43 cm
2001
EA2015.273
Sullivan Bequest

Seal: 磊磊画印 *Leilei huayin*

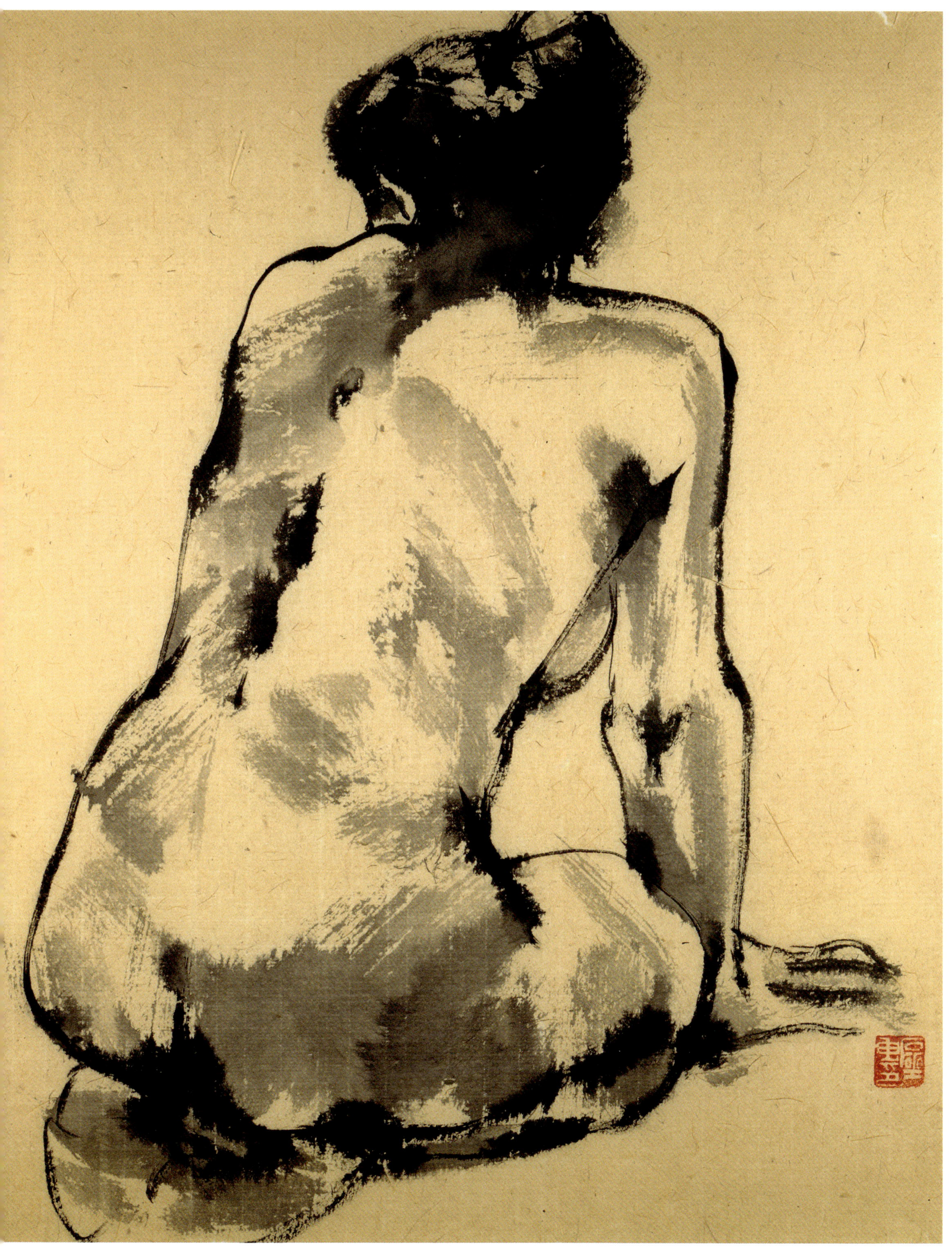

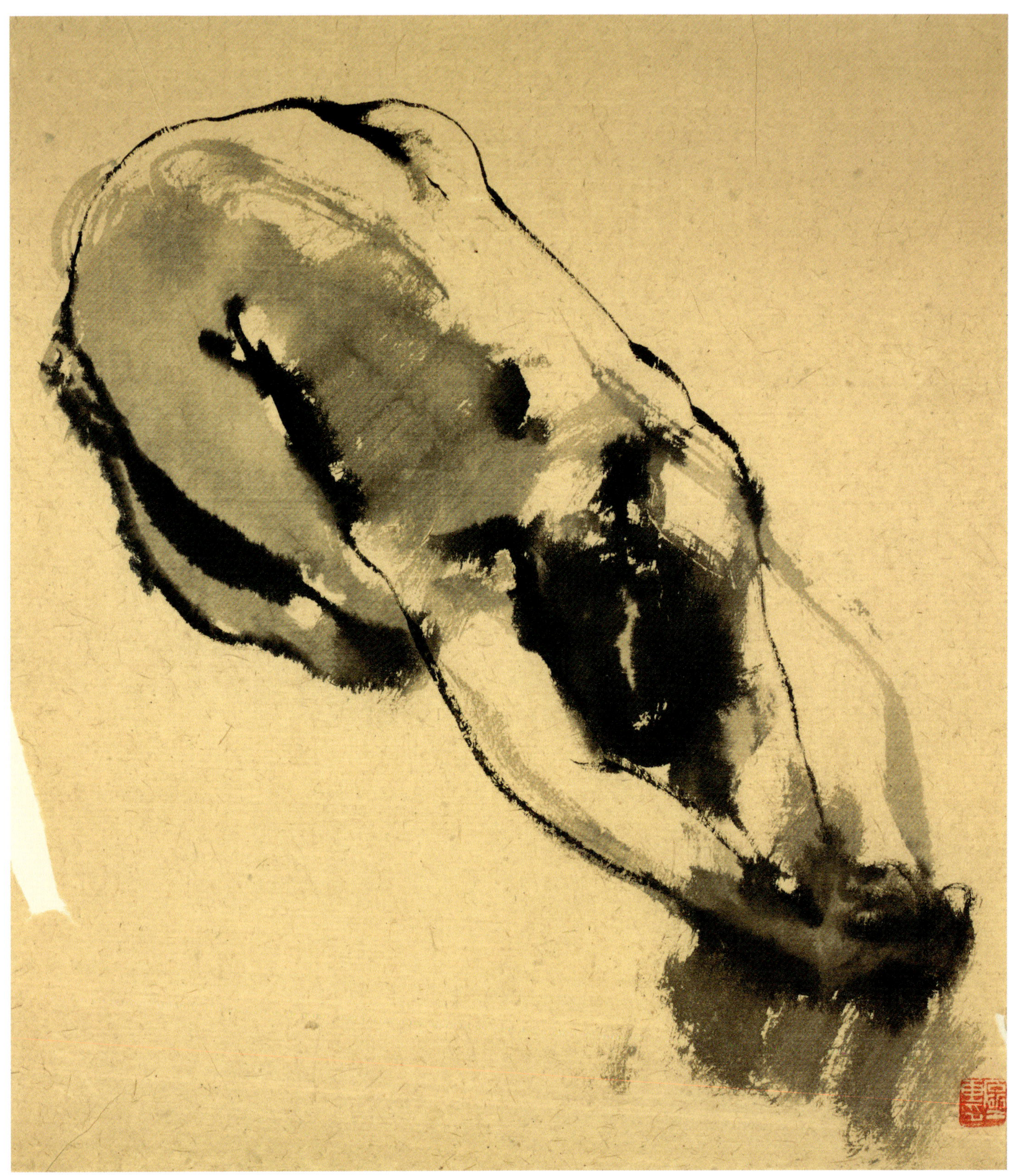

8
Reclining Figure
Ink on paper
46 × 42 cm
1997
Collection of the artist

Seal: 磊磊画印 *Leilei huayin*

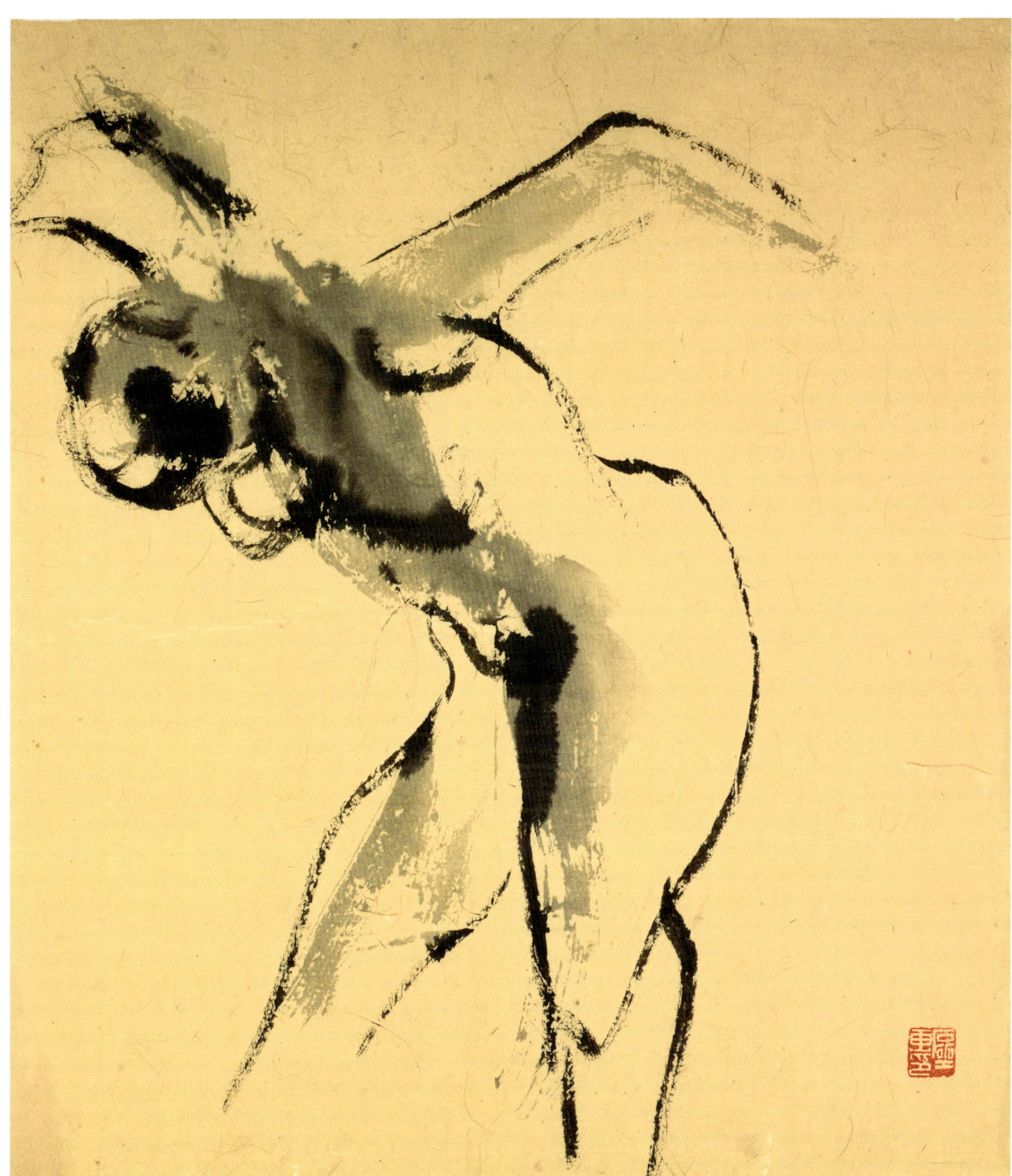

9
Dancing Figure
Ink on paper
46 × 42 cm
2014
Collection of the artist

Seal: 磊磊画印 *Leilei huayin*

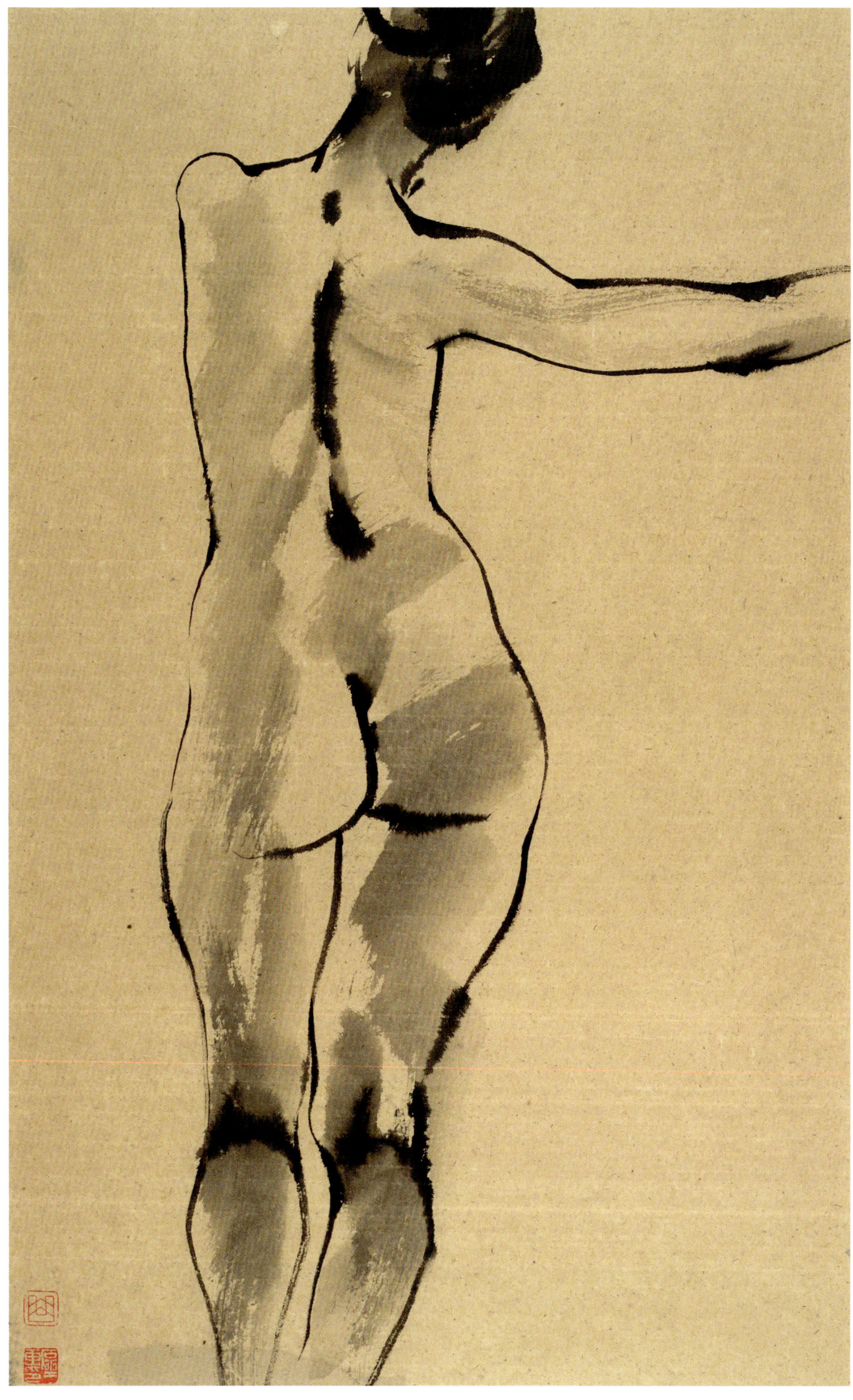

10
Standing Figure I
Ink on paper
77 × 48 cm
2014
Collection of the artist

Seal 1:曲Qu
Seal 2: 磊磊画印 Leilei huayin

11
Standing Figure II
Ink on paper
82.5 × 53 cm
2014
Collection of the artist

Seal 1:曲 Qu
Seal 2: 磊磊画印 *Leilei huayin*

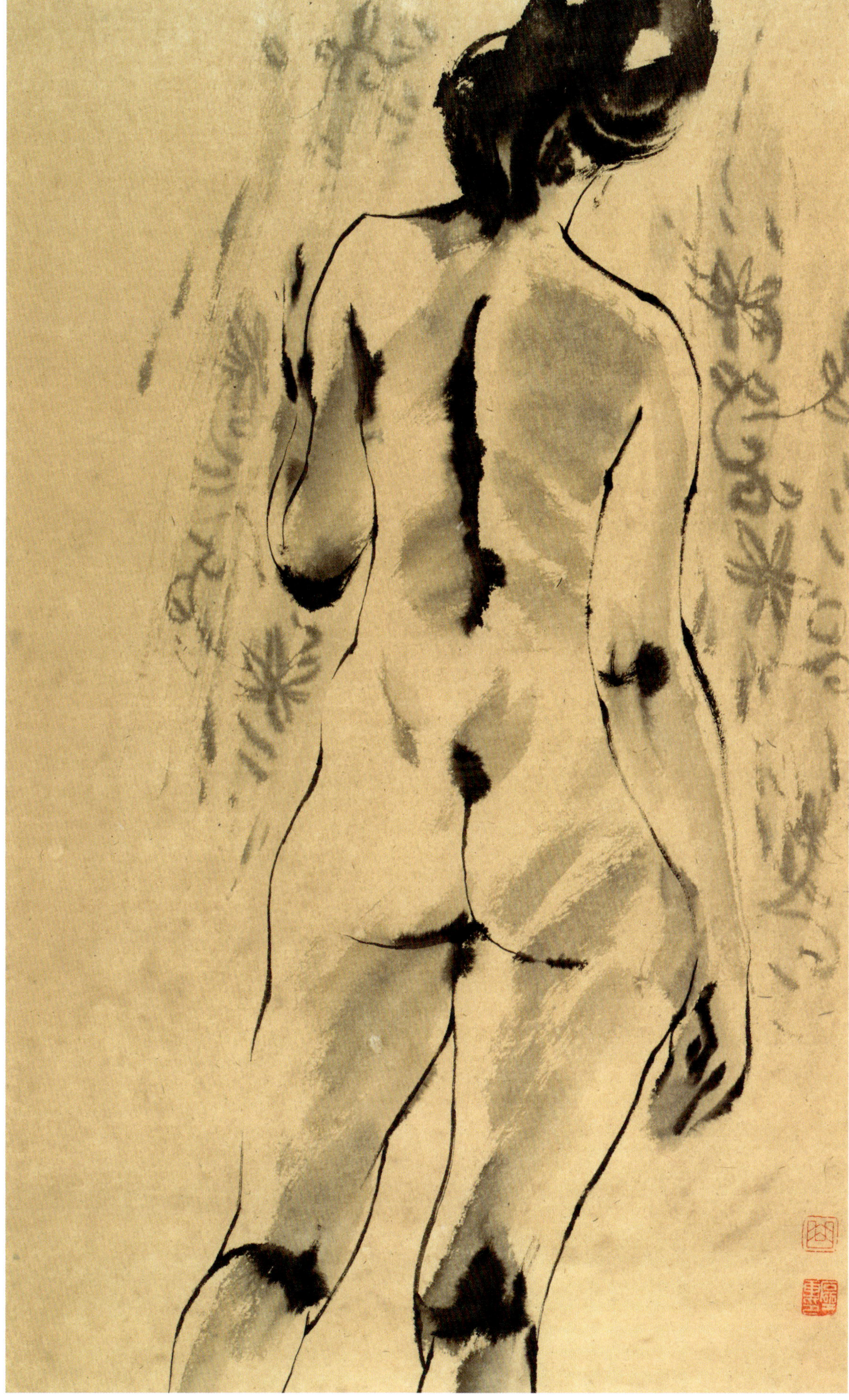

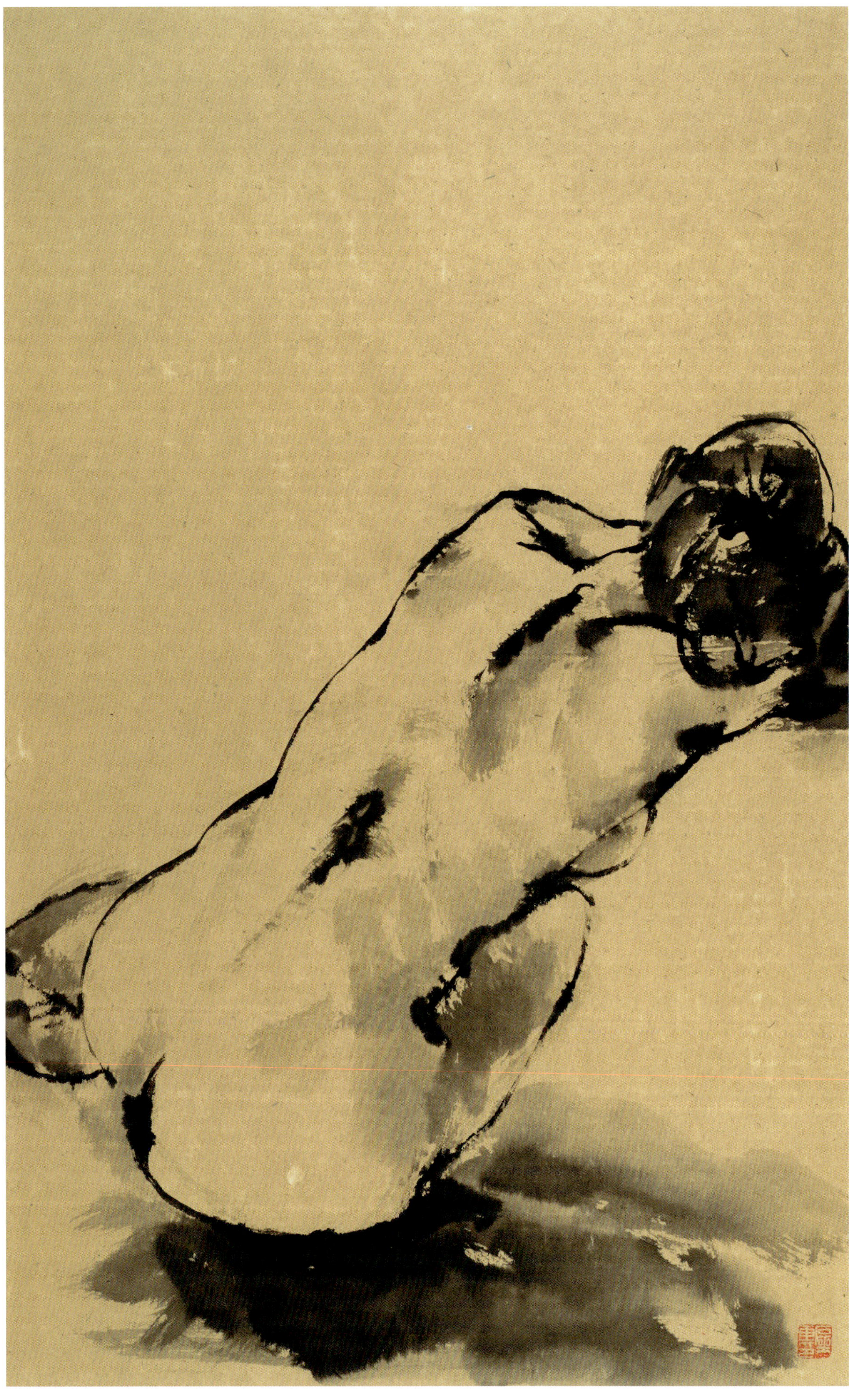

12
Seated Figure
Ink on paper
82.5 × 53 cm
2012
Collection of the artist

Seal: 磊磊画印 *Leilei huayin*

13

Balance
Ink and colour wash on paper
31 × 28 cm
2012
Collection of the artist

Seal: 曲 *Qu*

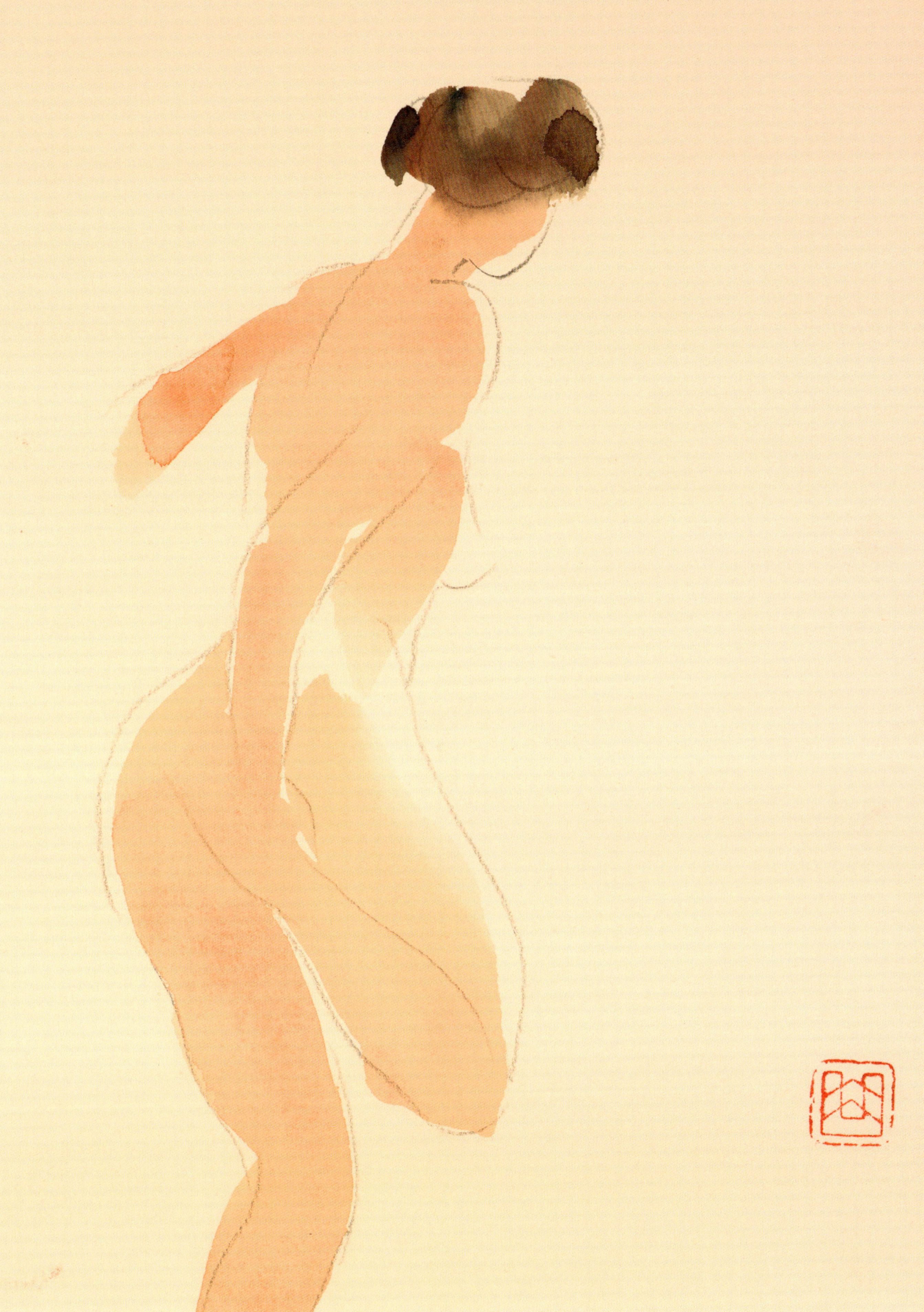

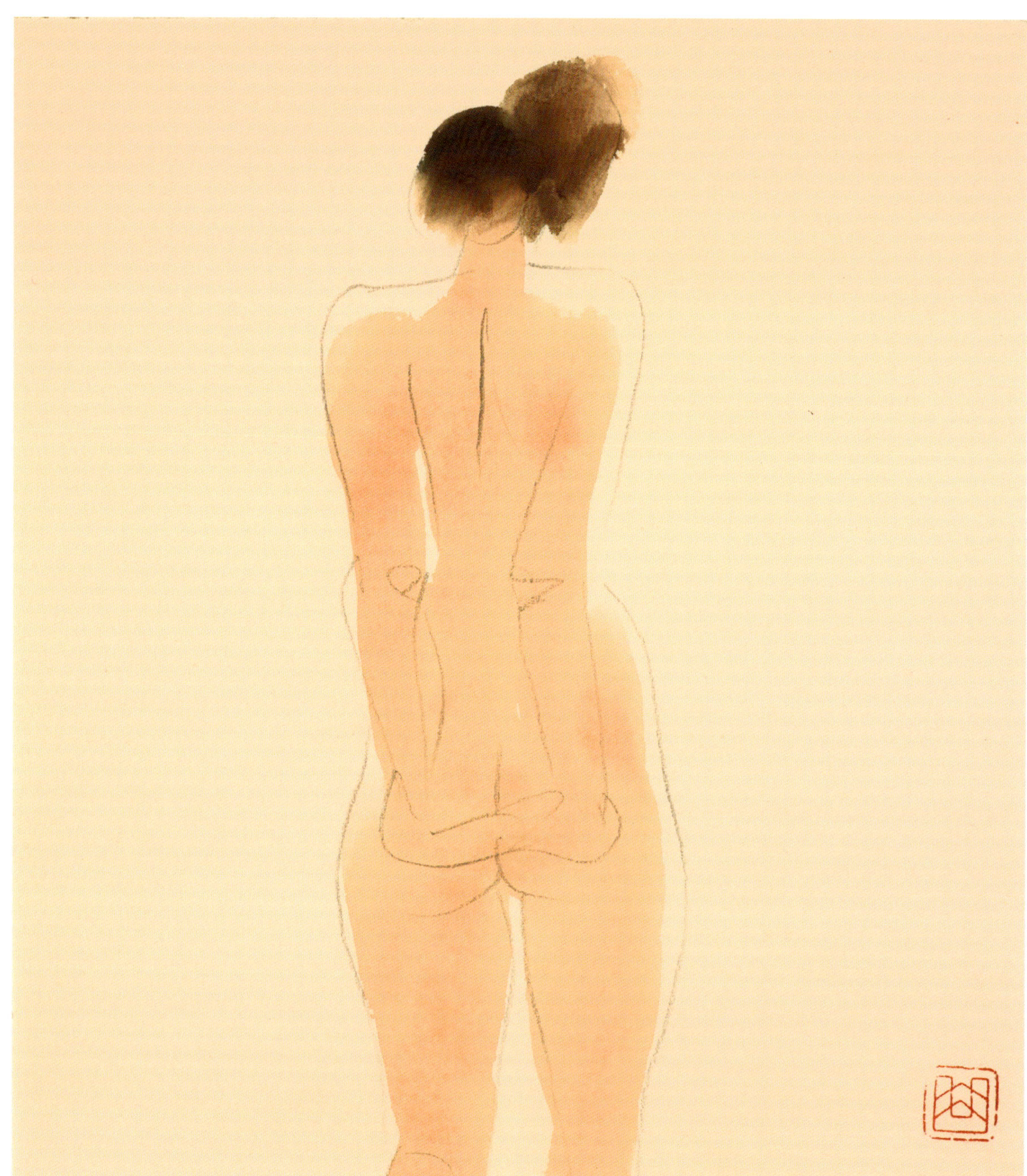

14
Figure Outstretched
Ink and colour wash on paper
31 × 28 cm
2012
Collection of the artist

Seal: 曲 *Qu*

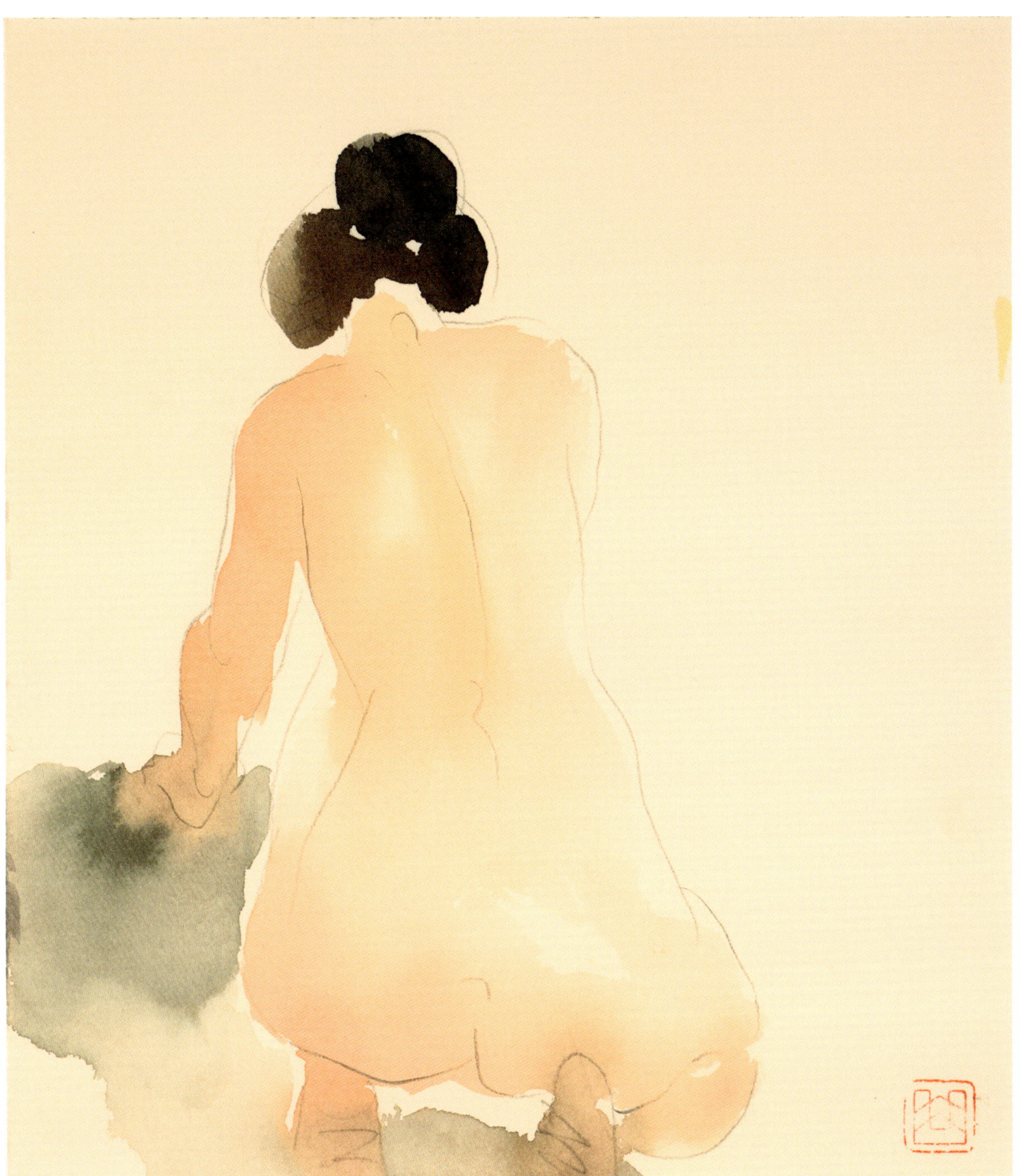

15
Figure Bending
Ink and colour wash on paper
31 × 28 cm
2012
Collection of the artist

Seal: 曲 *Qu*

16
Figure in Repose
Ink and colour wash on paper
31 × 28 cm
2012
Collection of the artist

Seal: 曲 *Qu*

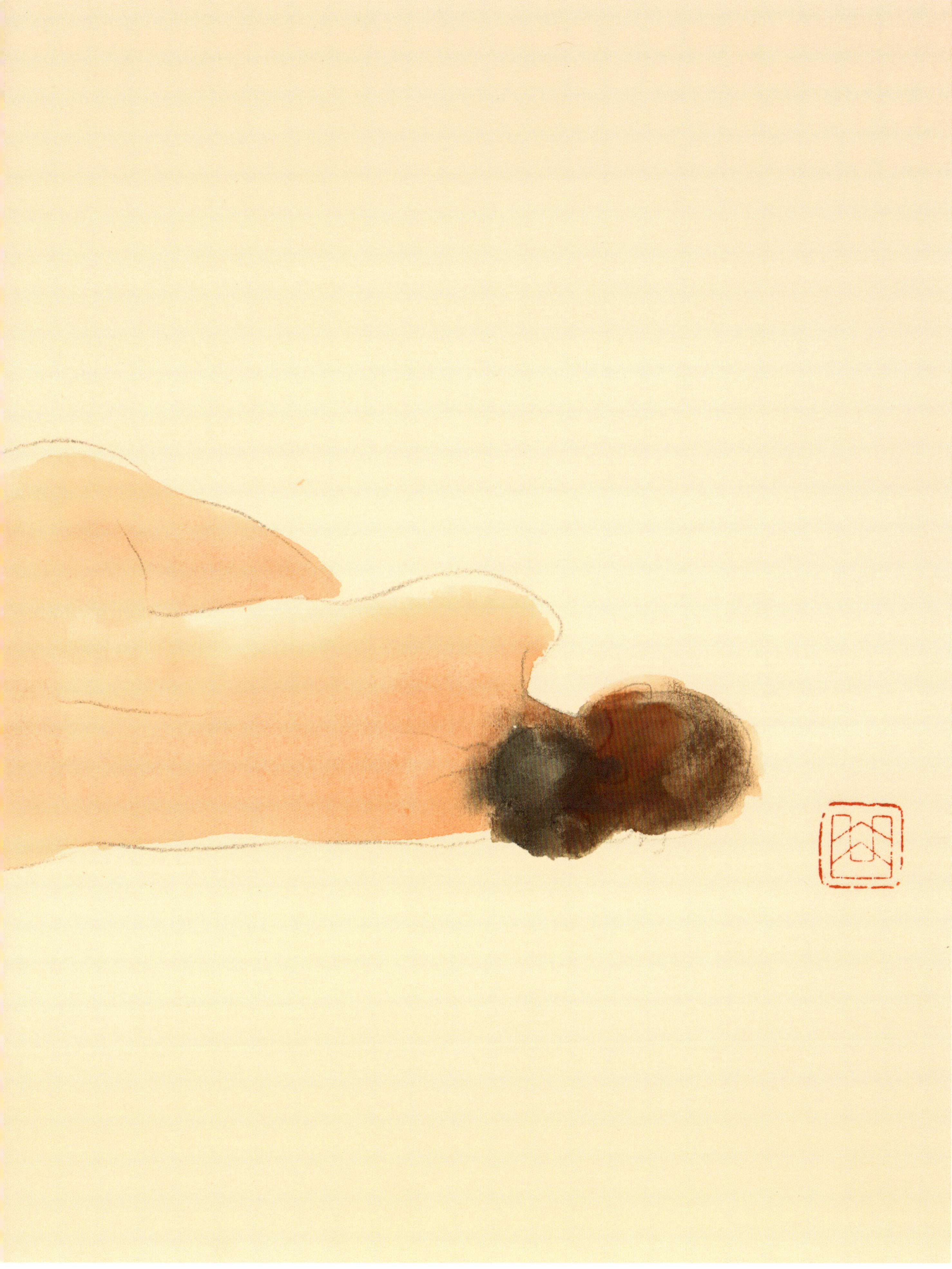

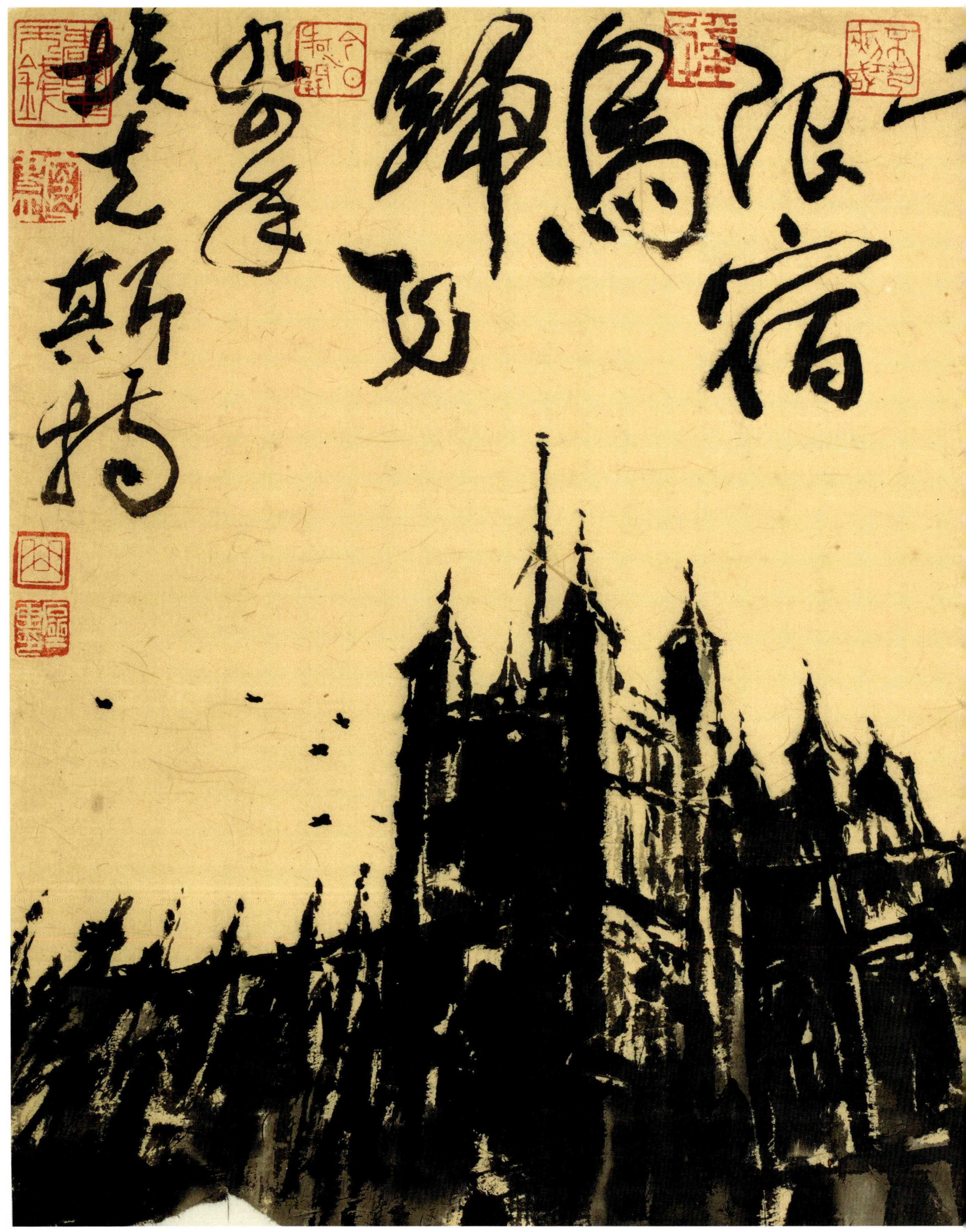

17
Exeter Cathedral
Ink on paper
46 × 42 cm
1994
Collection of the artist

Seal 1: 今日荷開 *Jinri hekai*
Seal 2: 囊中無錢 *Langzhong wuqian*
Seal 3: 雁北飛 *Yan bei fei*
Seal 4: 曲 *Qu*
Seal 5: 磊磊畫印 *Leilei huayin*

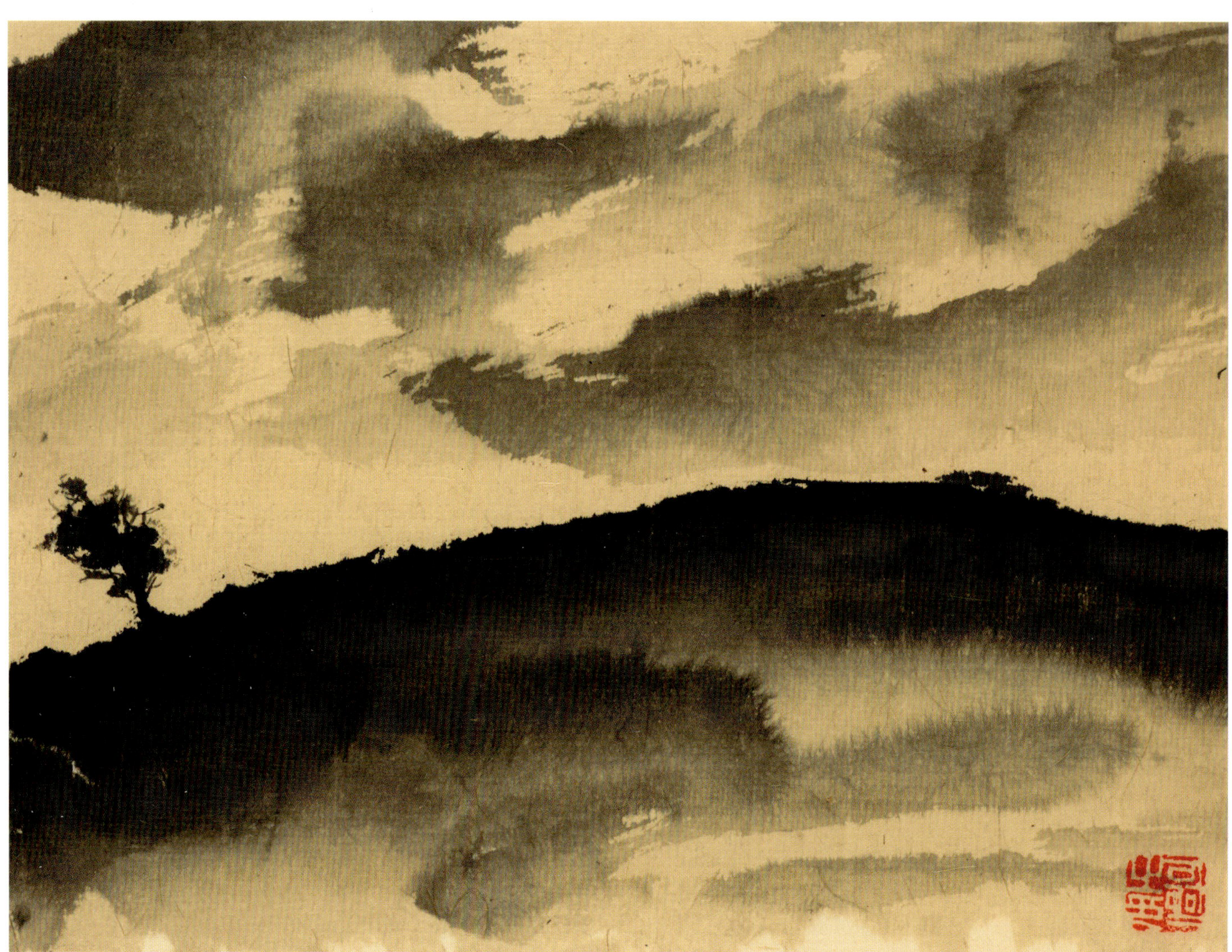

18
Spring
Ink on paper
16 × 22 cm
1992
Collection of the artist

Seal: 磊磊之印 *Leilei zhiyin*

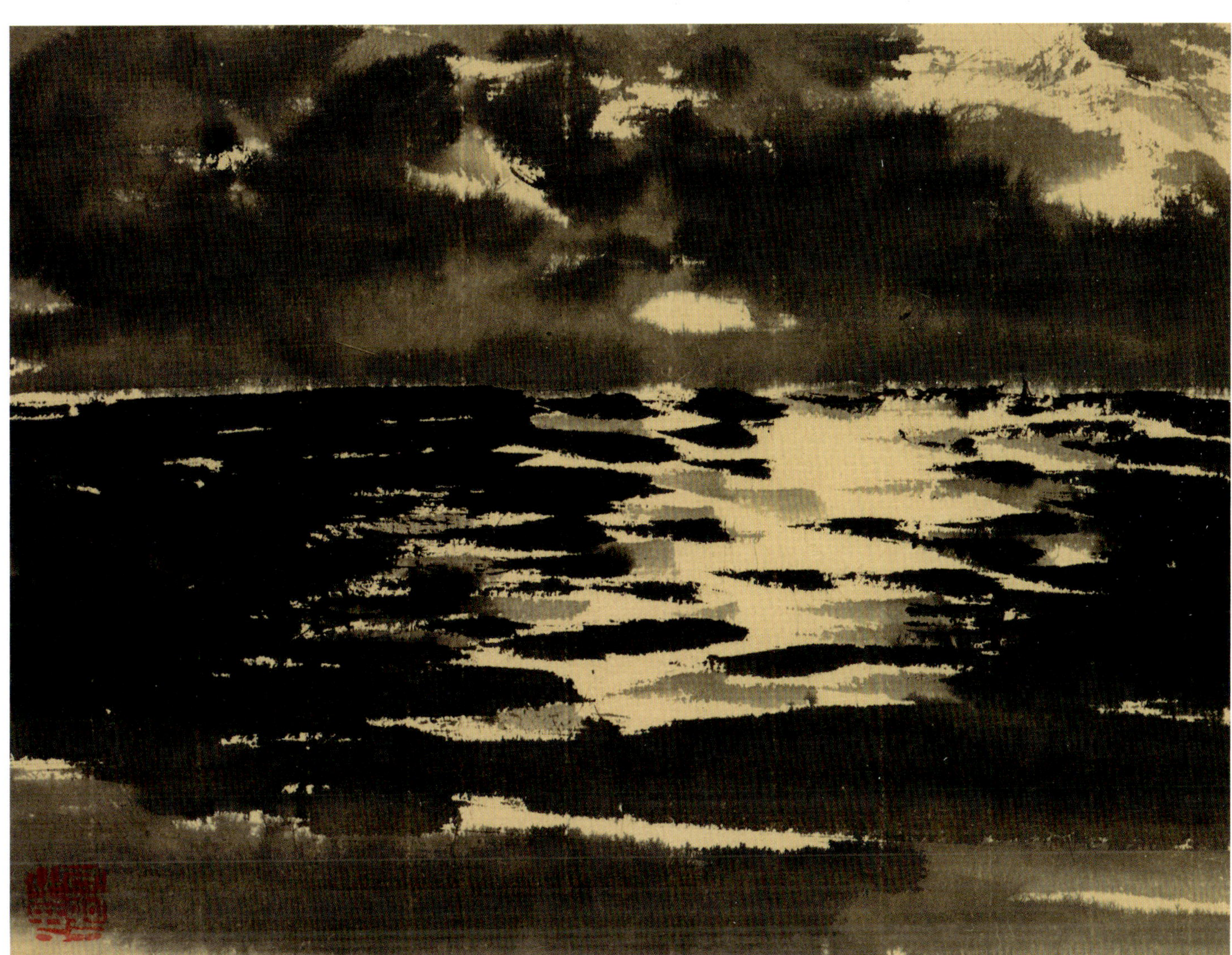

19
Summer
Ink on paper
16 × 22 cm
1992
Collection of the artist

Seal: 磊磊之印 *Leilei zhiyin*

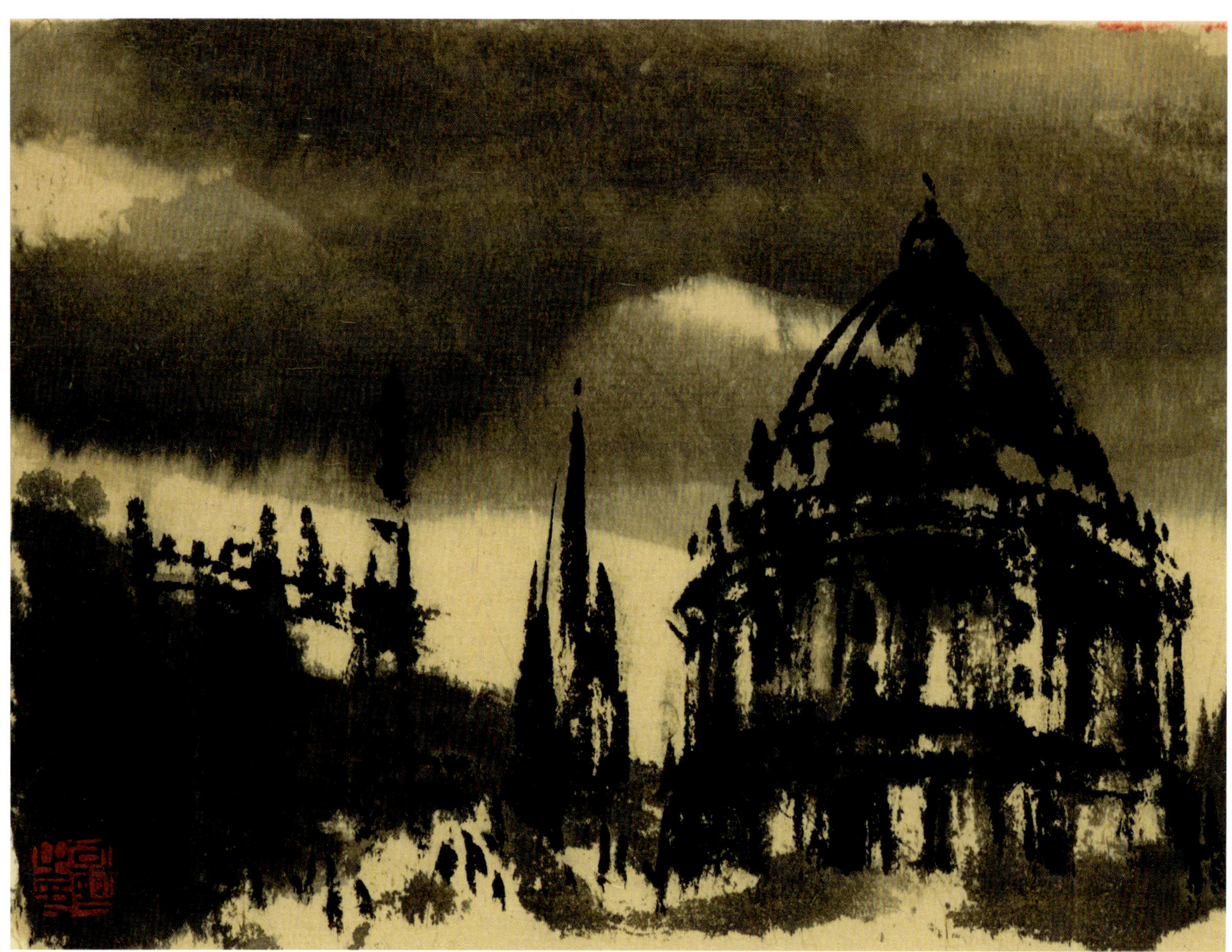

20
Autumn
Ink on paper
16 × 22 cm
2016
Collection of the artist

Seal: 磊磊之印 *Leilei zhiyin*

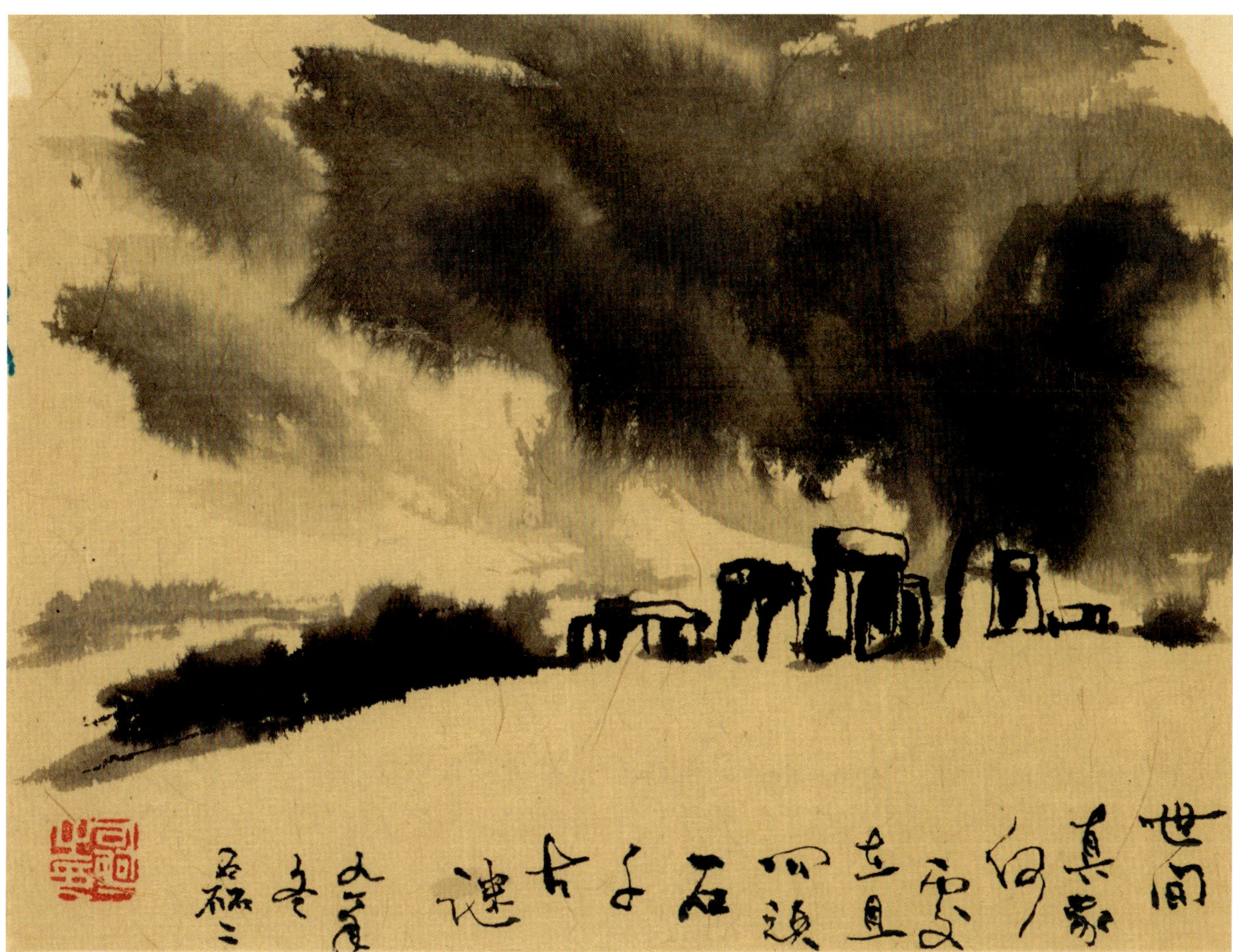

21
Winter
Ink on paper
16 × 22 cm
1991
Collection of the artist

Inscription:
世間真象何處在 且回頭 石千古謎 九一年冬 磊磊
'Where is the truth of the world? Looking back, thousands of years of mystery in Stonehenge. Leilei painted this in the winter of 1991.'

Seal: 磊磊畫印 *Leilei huayin*

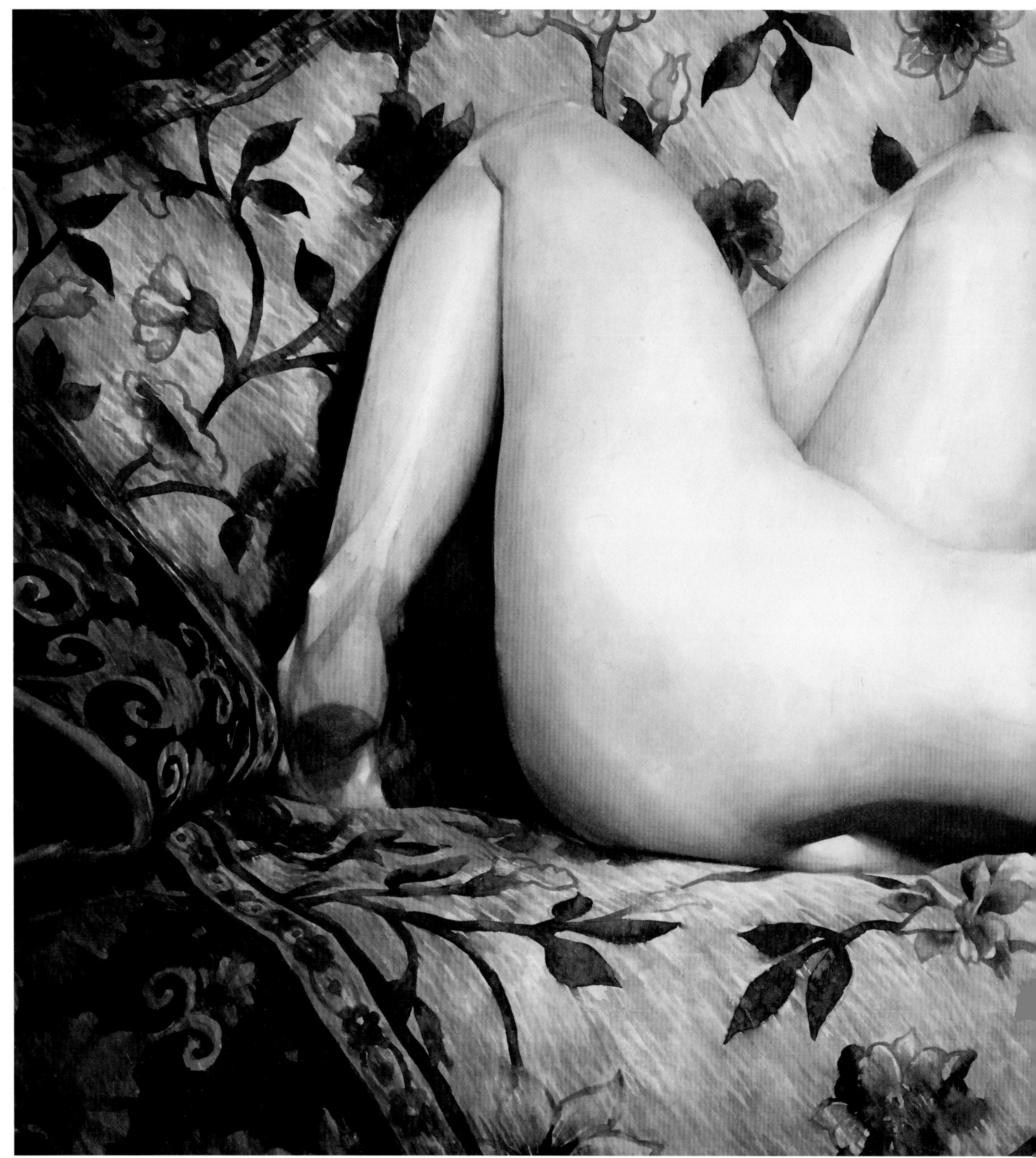

22
Reclining Nude (Danaë)
Ink on paper
89 × 168 cm
2016
Collection of the artist

Seal : 磊磊畫印 *Leilei huayin*

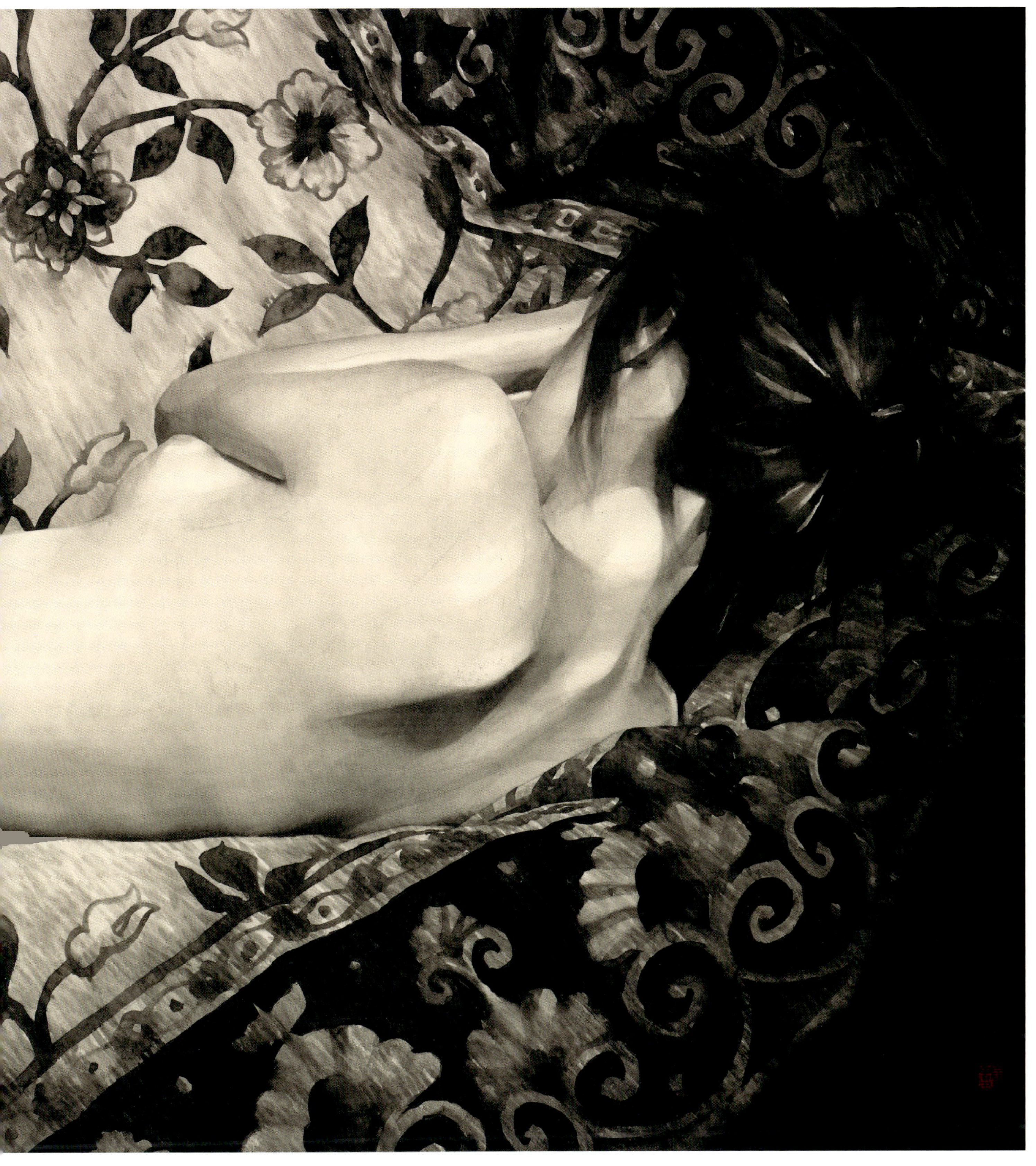

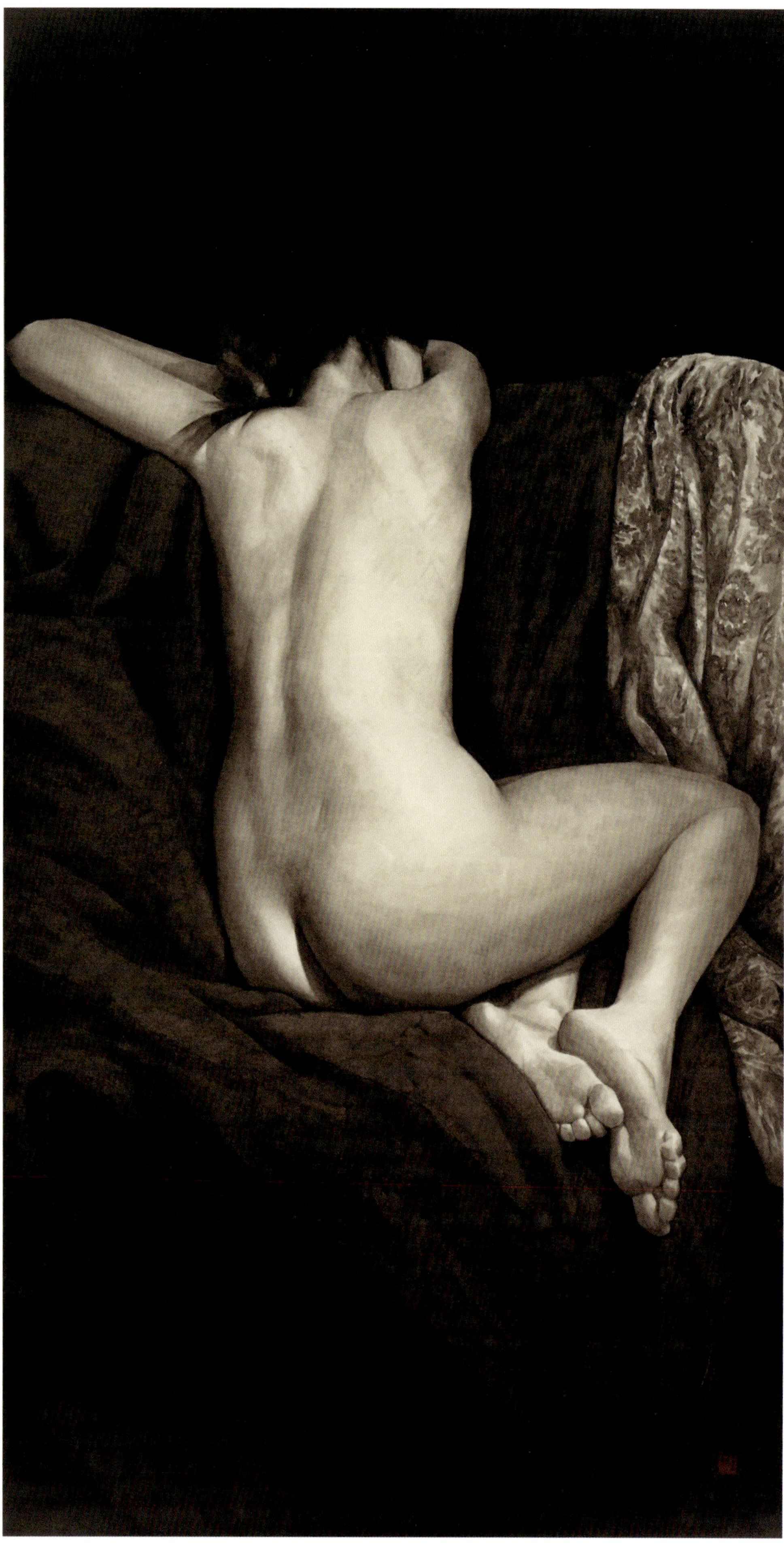

23
Seated Nude
Ink on paper
168 × 89 cm
2010
EA2015.277
Sullivan Bequest

Signature: 磊磊十年
Leilei painted in 2010

Seal 1: 曲 *Qu*
Seal 2: 磊磊畫印 *Leilei huayin*

24
Standing Nude
Ink on paper
170 × 92 cm
2016
Collection of the artist

Seal 1: 曲 *Qu*
Seal 2: 磊磊畫印 *Leilei huayin*

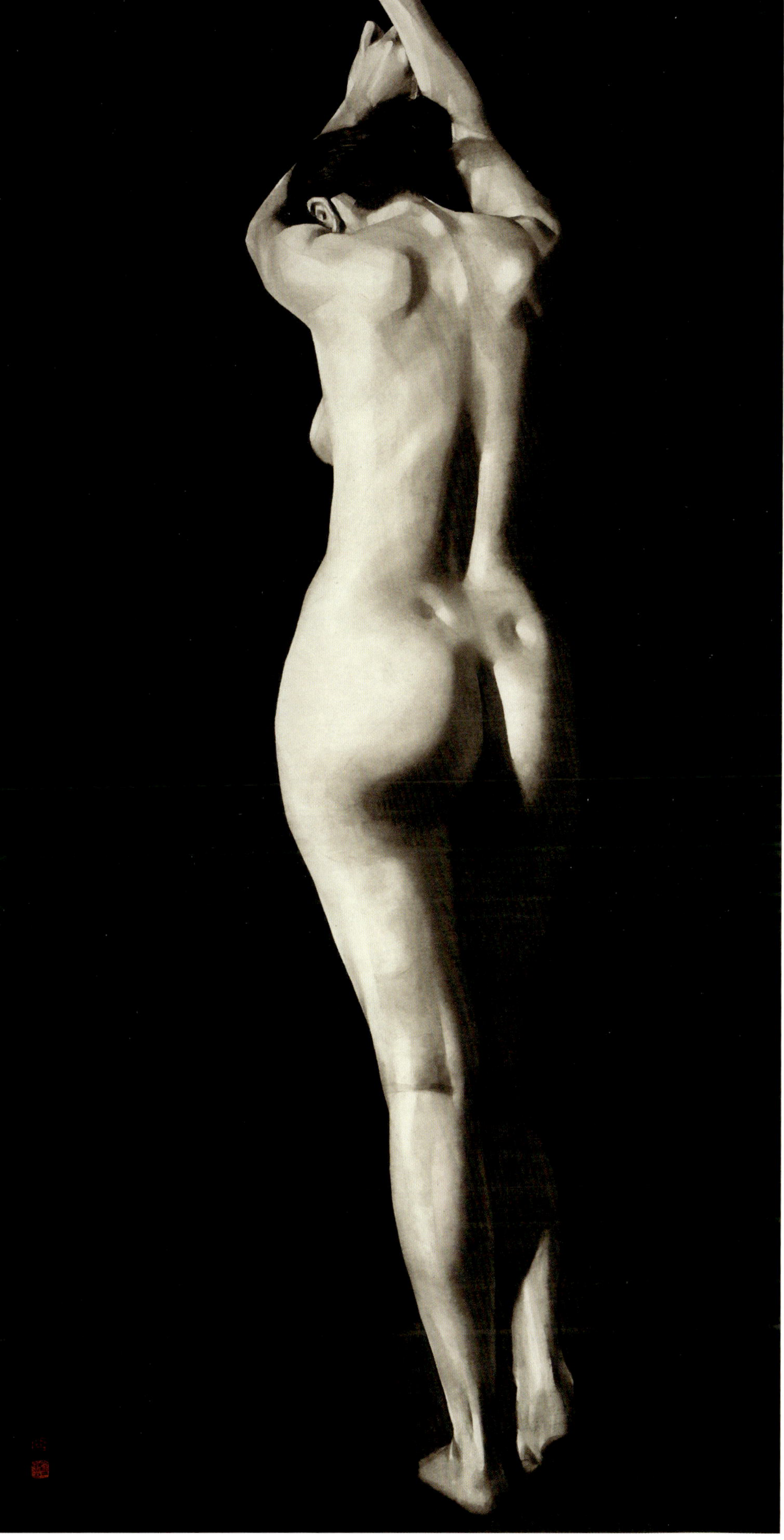

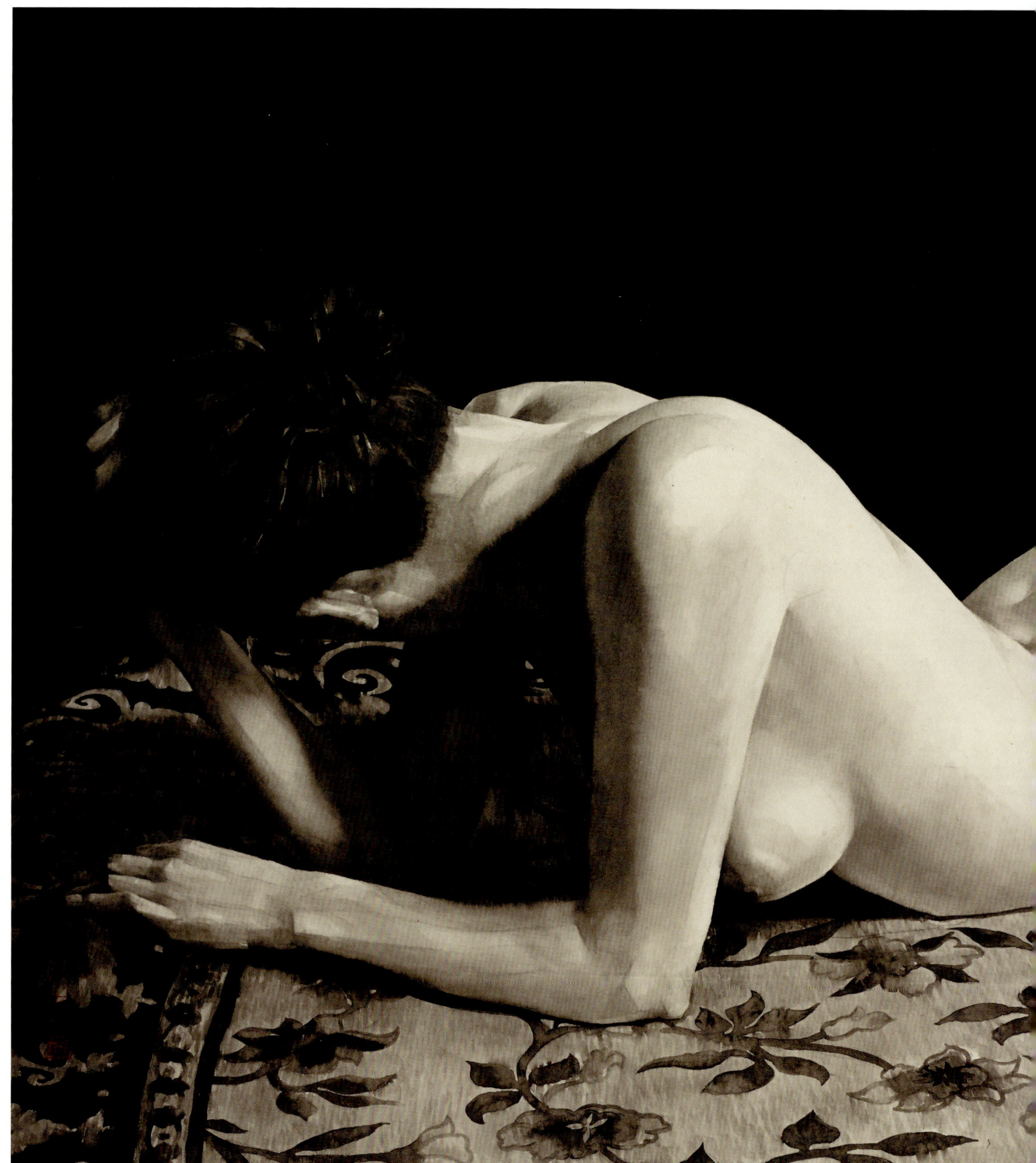

25
Reclining Nude
Ink on paper
92 × 170 cm
2016
Collection of the artist

Seal 1: 曲 *Qu*
Seal 2: 磊磊畫印 *Leilei huayin*
Seal 3: 大雅 *Da ya*

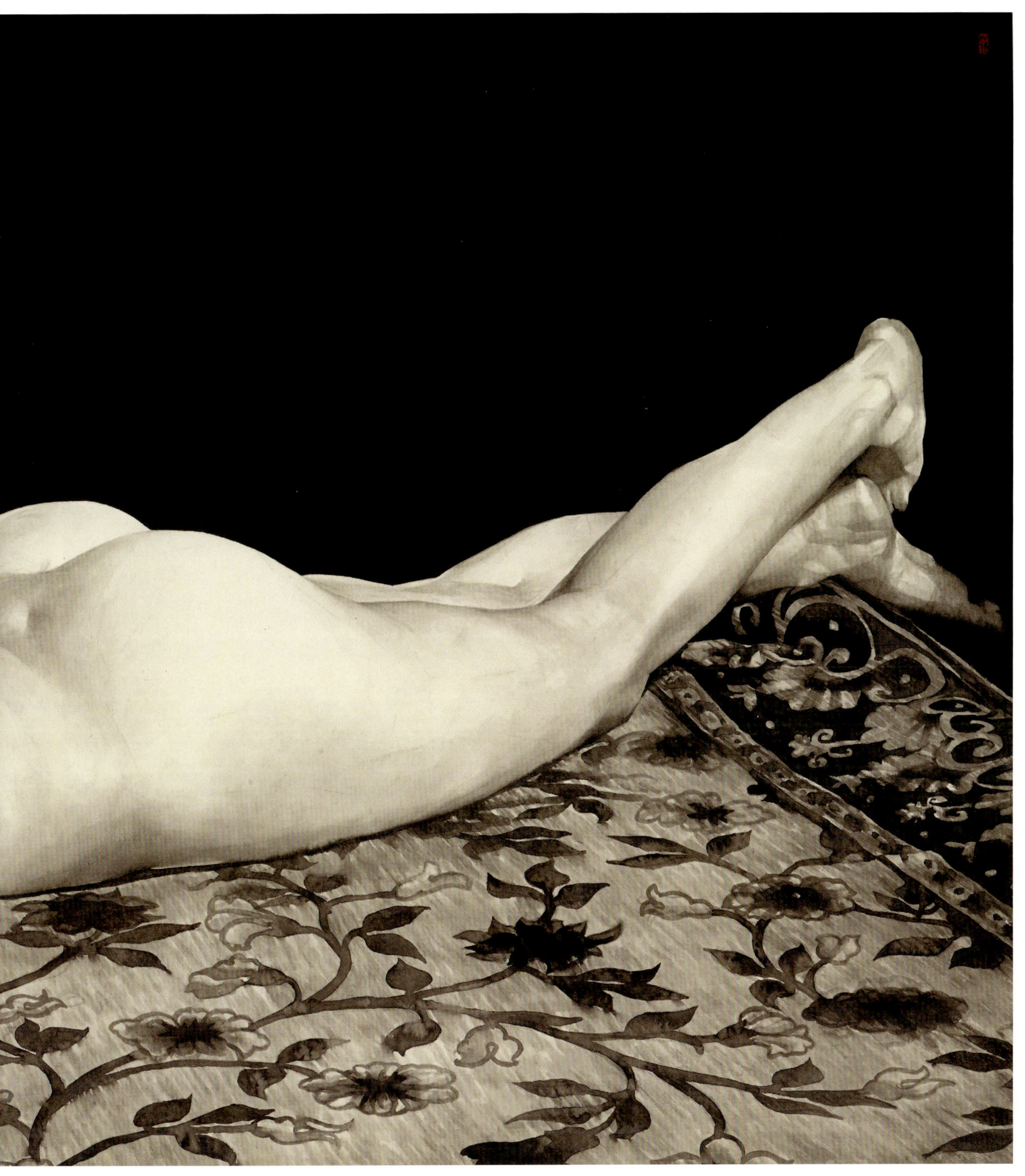

26

The Future Remains in Our Own Hands
Ink on paper
90 × 122 cm
2014
Collection of the artist

Seal 1: 曲 *Qu*
Seal 2: 磊磊畫印 *Leilei huayin*
Seal 3: 大雅 *Da ya*

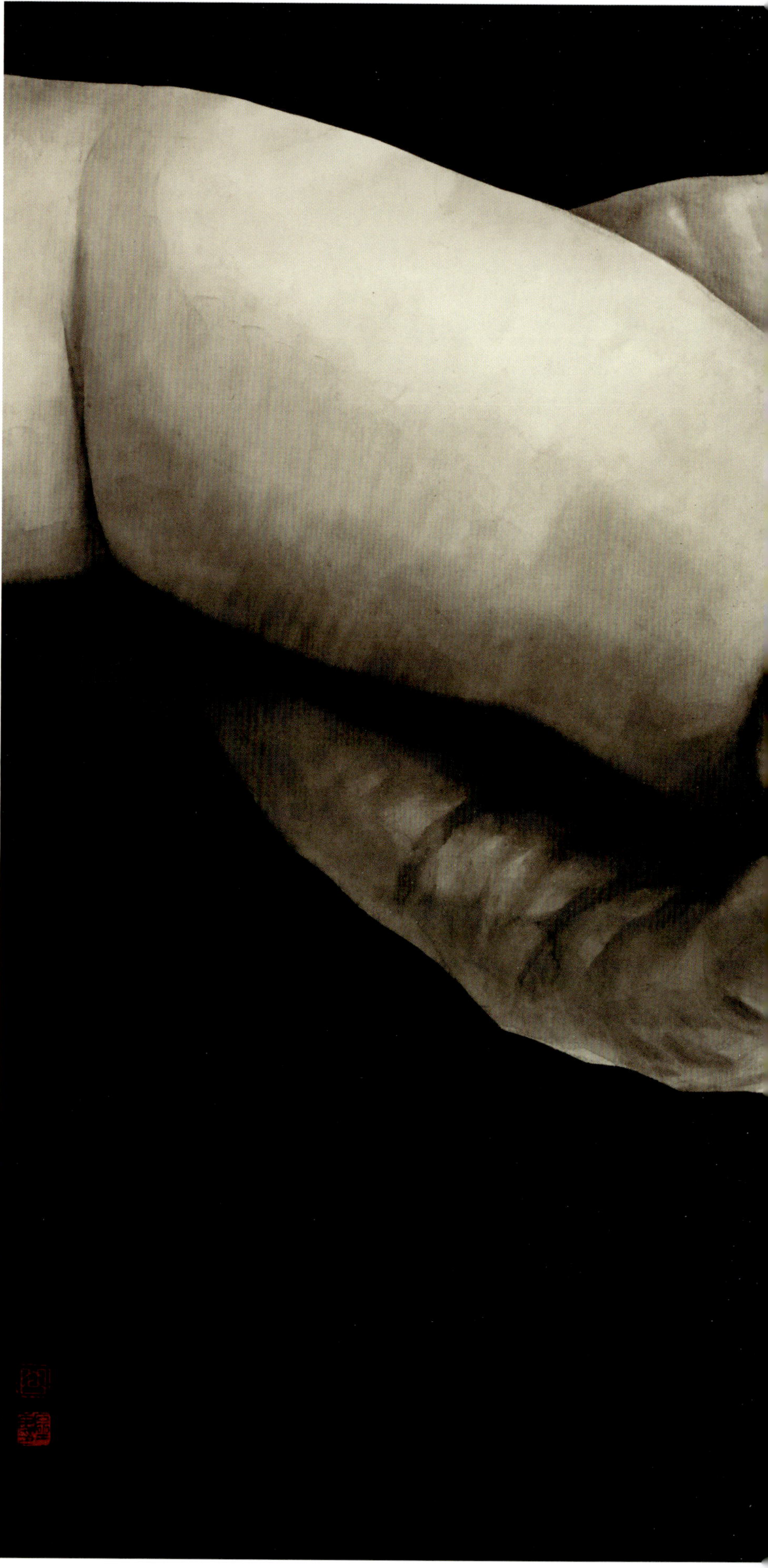

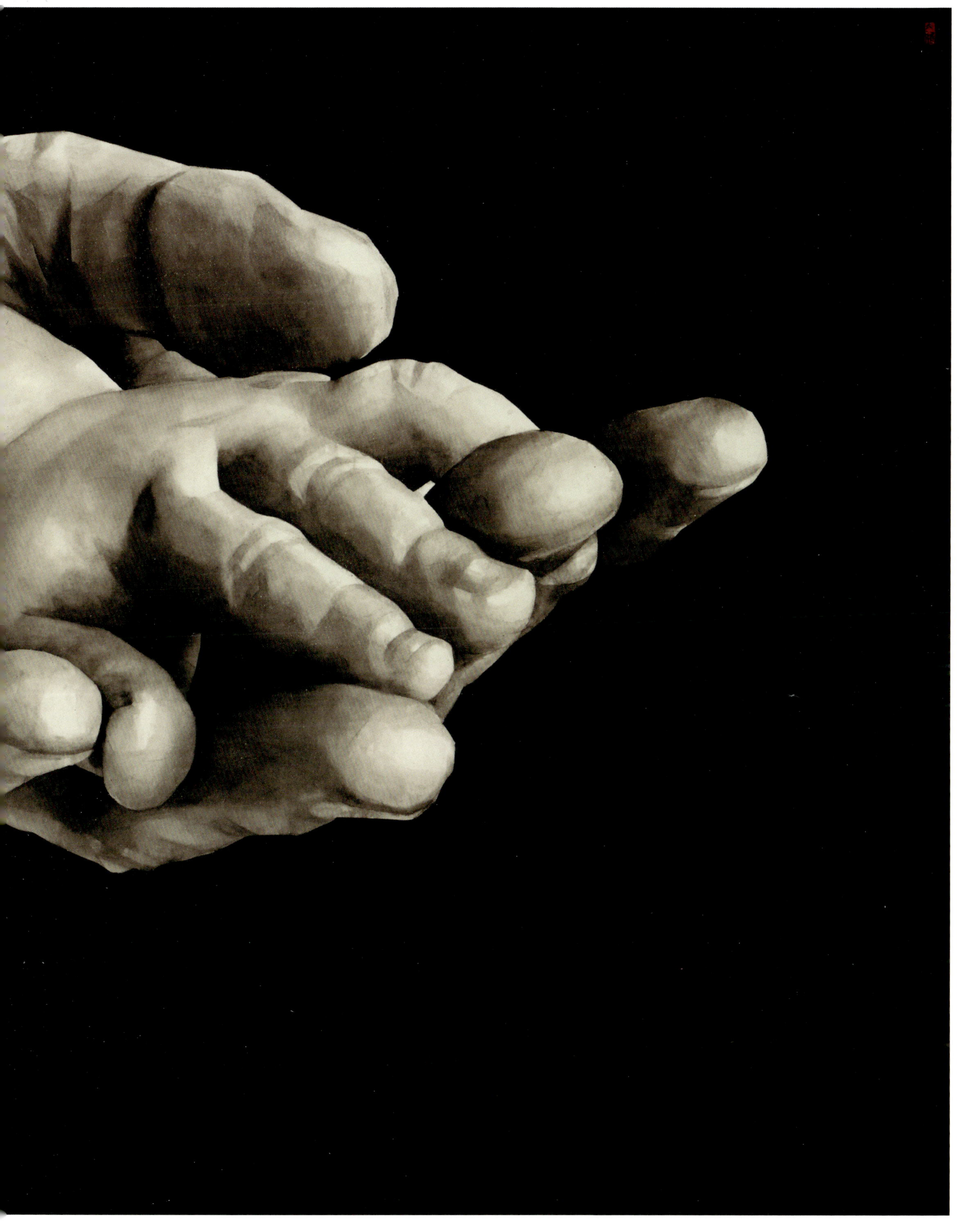

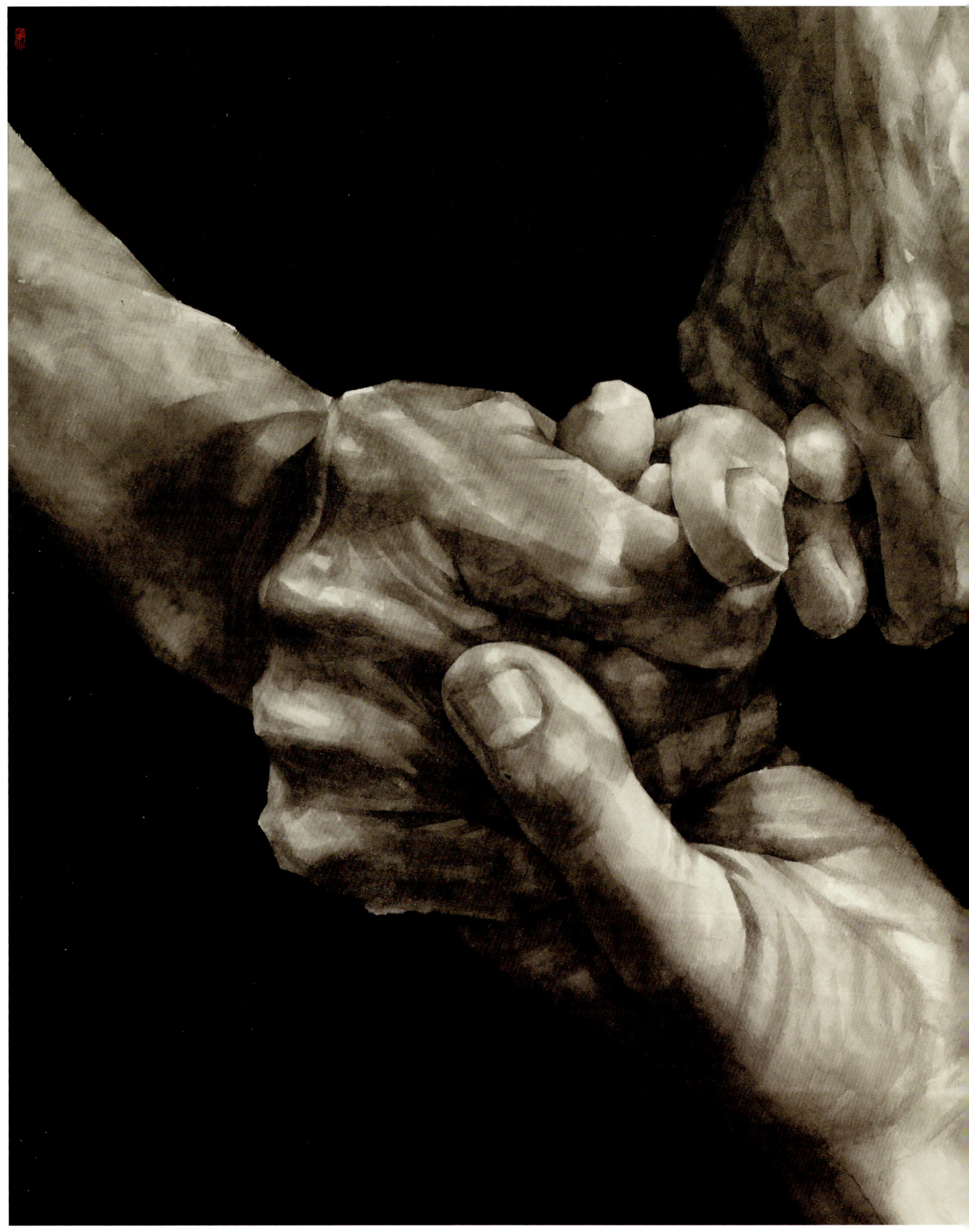

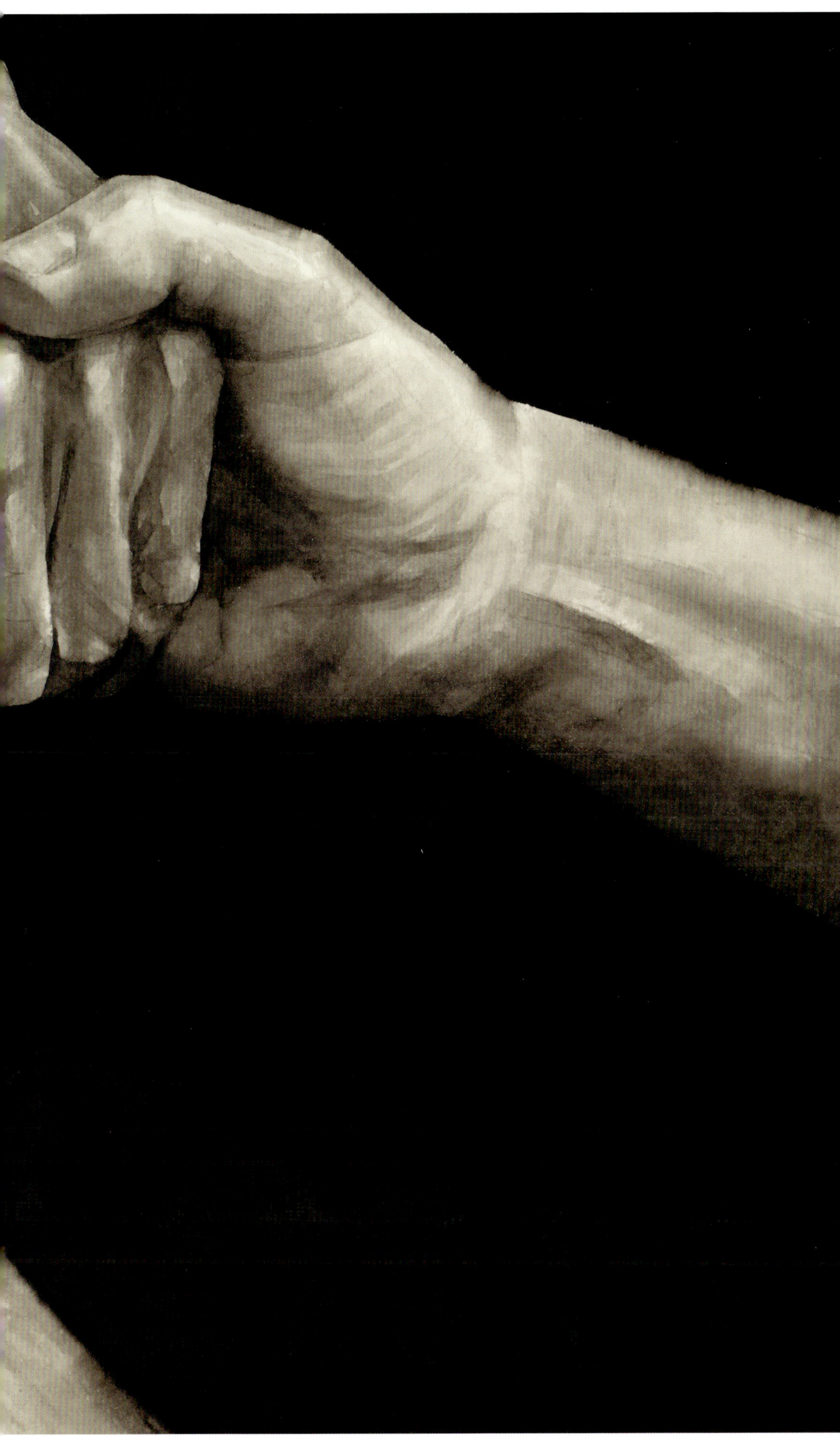

27
Friendship
Ink on paper
90 × 186 cm
2012
Collection of the artist

Seal 1: 曲 *Qu*
Seal 2: 磊磊畫印 *Leilei huayin*

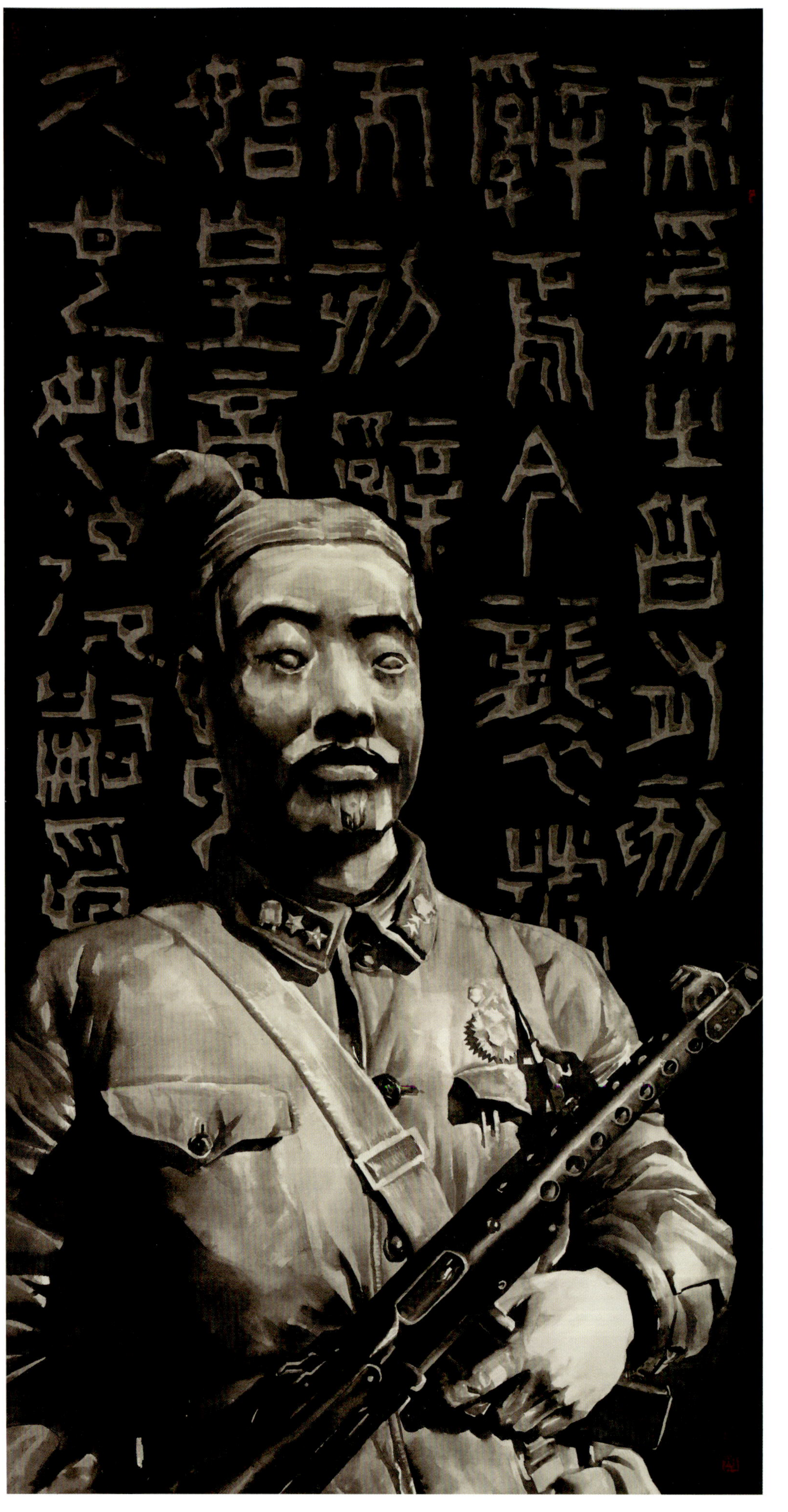

28
The Soldier
Ink on paper
170 × 90 cm
2013
Collection of the artist

Signature: 磊磊一三年
Leilei painted in 2013

Seal 1: 曲 *Qu*
Seal 2: 磊磊畫印 *Leilei huayin*

29 (overleaf)
The Invincible
Ink on paper
92 × 170 cm
2015
Collection of the artist

Signature: 磊磊 *Leilei*

Seal: 磊磊畫印 *Leilei huayin*

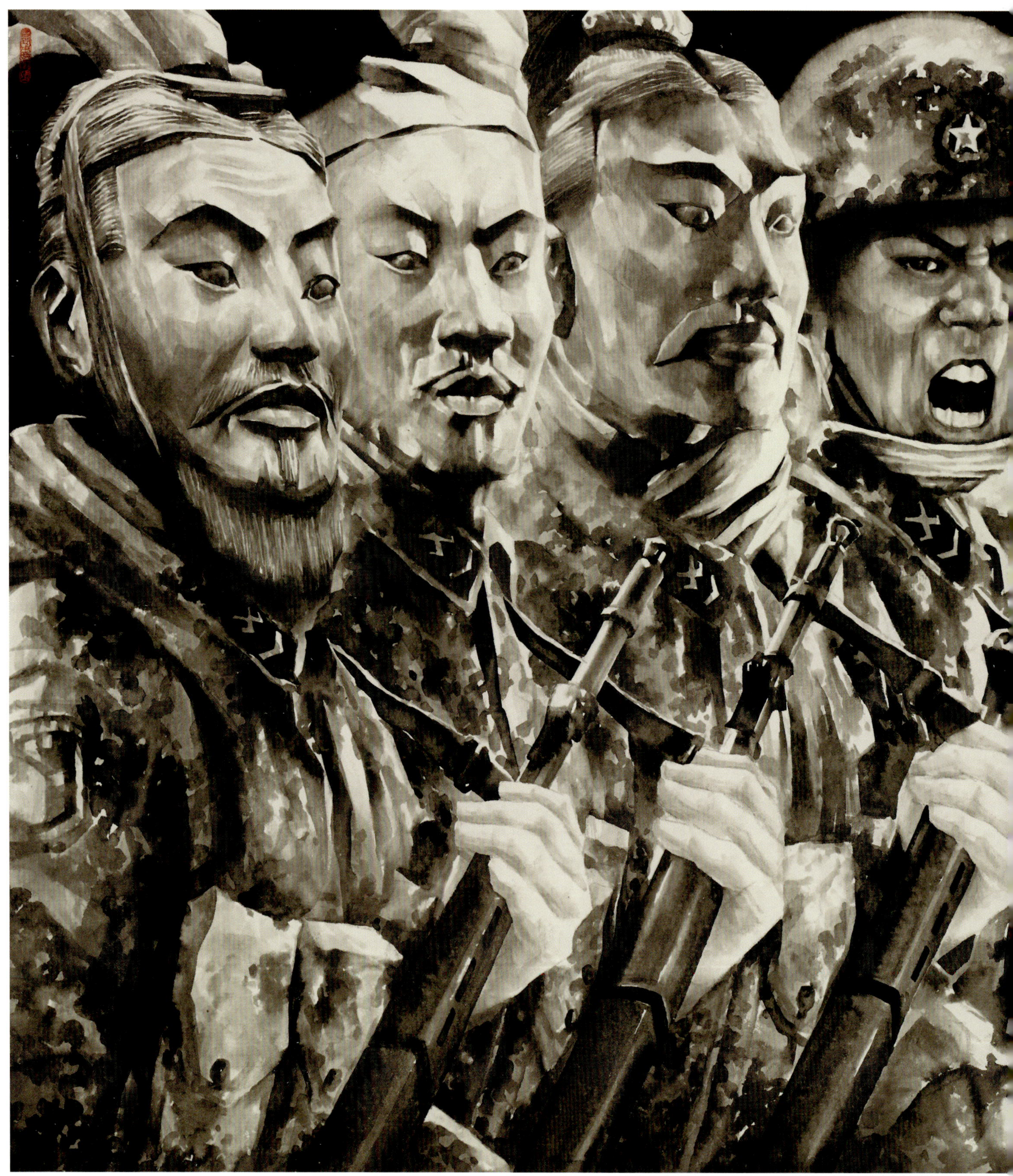

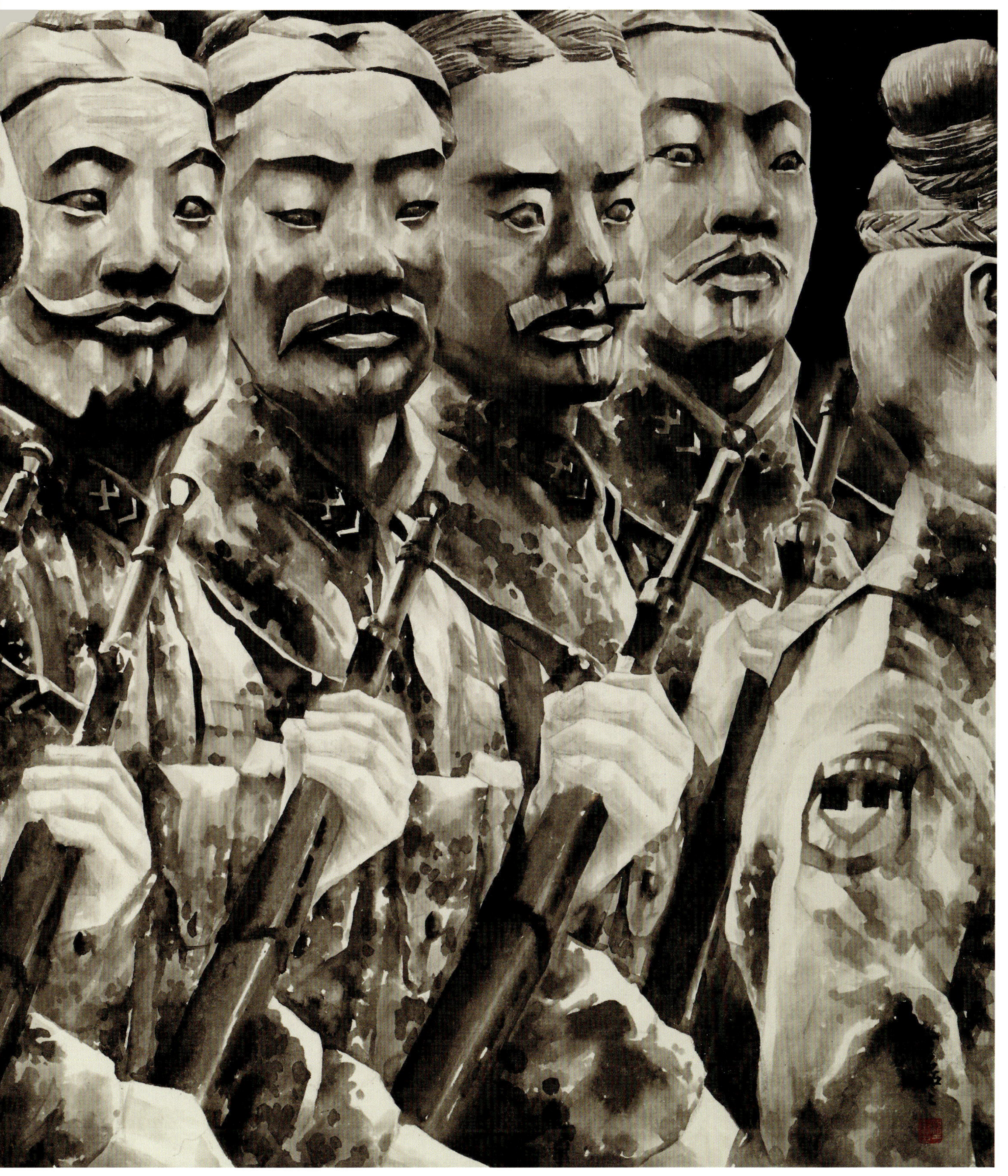

Chronology

1951	Born in HeiLongJiang, China
1958–64	Studied traditional Chinese painting and calligraphy under Tan Wancun
1977–8	Studied human anatomy at Beijing Medical University
1985	Moved to London
1986–8	Studied Western art under Cecil Collins at the Central School of Art, London
1990–present	Lecturer in Chinese art at Sotheby's Institute, London
2000–present	President of British Chinese Brush Painters Society

Major museum exhibitions

2017	'enLIGHTENMENT', solo show, 3812 Gallery, Hong Kong
2015	'Hand Series and Lei Feng', joint exhibition with Ma Desheng, The British Museum
	'Silent Revelations', solo show, Hua Gallery, London
2014	'Modern Brush and Ink', solo show, Galerie Frank Pages, Geneva
2011	'Brush, Ink, Light, Shadow', solo show, The National Art Museum of China, Beijing
2009	Solo show, Leda Fletcher Gallery, Geneva
2008	'Brush, Ink, Light, Shadow', solo show, Littleton & Hennessy Asian Art, New York
2007	'Brush, Ink, Light, Shadow', solo show, Leda Fletcher Gallery, Shanghai
2006	Solo show, Campbell Gallery, South Kensington, London
2005	The second Beijing Biennale, Beijing, China
	'Everyone's Life is an Epic', solo show, The Ashmolean, University of Oxford
2004	'Art on Paper', Blunden Oriental, Royal College of Art, London
2003	Joint exhibition with Caroline Deane, The Aldeburgh Gallery, Suffolk
2002	Solo show, Galerie Leda Fletcher, Geneva
2001	'The Paragon', solo show, The Cape of Good Hope Gallery, Singapore
	49th Biennale Di Venezia, Venice, Italy
2000	Solo show, Galerie Leda Fletcher, Geneva
	'Art Towards Reconciliation', The Guernica Museum, Spain
	The 'Stars' 20th Anniversary Exhibition, Tokyo, Japan
1999	'Here and Now – to Face a New Century', solo show, The Truman Brewery Gallery, London
	48th Biennale Di Venezia, Venice, Italy
	'Nude', solo show, The Redfern Gallery, London
1998	'Chinese Contemporary Art' Mountboron Castle, Beaumount-en-Beine, France
	'5000+1', Bilbao, Spain
1997	Solo show, Chinese Contemporary Gallery, London
	'Far From Shore', Pitshanger Manor and Gallery, London
1996	'Contemporary Chinese Art', Galleri Asur, Oslo, Norway
	'Fine Chinese Work of Art', Christie's, Paris
1995	Joint exhibition, The Blue Gallery, London
1993	'East Going West', solo show, Tricycle Gallery, London
1992	'Linear Rhythm', solo show, Calligraphy exhibition, The Central Gallery, Covent Garden, London
1991	Solo show, Barclays Business Centre, Covent Garden, London
1989	'Never Forget', Pompidou Centre, Paris
	'The 'Stars' 10th Anniversary Exhibition ', Hanart Gallery, Hong Kong and TaiPei
1987	'Contemporary Chinese Art', Royal Festival Hall, London
1986	'East Meet West', Joint exhibition, Holland Gallery, London
1985	'National Ceramics' exhibition, Beijing, China
1980	The second 'Stars' Exhibition, Beijing, China
1979	The first 'Stars' Exhibition, Beijing, China